WHAT'S BOTHERING RASHI?

A GUIDE TO
IN-DEPTH ANALYSIS OF
HIS TORAH COMMENTARY

AVIGDOR BONCHEK

BEREISHIS

JERUSALEM FELDHEIM PUBLISHERS NEW YORK

First published 1997
ISBN 0-87306-849-1

FELDHEIM PUBLISHERS
200 Airport Executive Park
Nanuet, NY 10954

POB 35002 / Jerusalem, Israel

Printed in Israel

Designed & Produced by:
Laser Pages Publishing Ltd., Jerusalem
972-2-6522226

TALMUDICAL YESHIVA OF PHILADELPHIA

6063 Drexel Road
Philadelphia, Pennsylvania 19131
215 - 477 - 1000

Rabbi Elya Svei
Rabbi Shmuel Kamenetsky
Roshei Yeshiva

בעז"ה כ"ג לחודש אייר ולסדר

לכבוד ידידי היקר הרב ר' שלמה
הכהן ד"ולק שליט"א

אחדשה"ט דברים עמוקה זה לי זה...
את אשר יחד... כדי ראשון קצין לזה
לעיני את דברי זה על ל' ואיל... ואש... ולא
... ולעברי הרמב"ם ... כי... כך בעיני ...
... נכון כאשר יסוד... יפה ואש... מחדש...
... מהדיולוריות להדיולויות דבריו הק' על יד' ...
אריה ...ל ... יעבע ברוק על ...
... לשלוח ה ...וי ו...
... כי ...יל... ...כן הדרך ...

...

דודו ...אהב
שמואל ...

Rabbi Shmuel Kamenetsky

Rabbi Nachman Bulman
Yeshivat Ohr Somayach
Ohr Lagolah

הרב נחמן בולמן
ישיבת אור שמח
אור לגולה

בס"ד

כד' בניסן תשנ"ז

May 1, 1997

The writer of these lines has seen a notable new work on Rashi — "What's Bothering Rashi? A Guide to In-Depth Analysis of Rashi's Torah Commentary" by Avigdor Bonchek.

Students of Rashi are uniquely affected by his elemental simplicity of style. Children are indelibly stirred by his words, masters of Torah see in his words the heights of Torah genius. Over the centuries C'lal Yisroel sees Rashi as our companion in the eternal climb to Sinai. Commentary on Rashi has been as limitless as our people's preoccupation with Torah.

Central to the Torah revival of our time has therefore also been Rashi-commentary in English — except for one characteristic of classical Rashi learning; namely that Rashi learning "put us" as it were into his laboratory. We asked with him, we probed with him, we lived his solution. He took us to Sinai again with him.

R. Bonchek's work again takes us, as it were, into Rashi's cheder and Beis HaMedrash. He puts "us into Rashi" and not just "Rashi into us." Many will be grateful to him for his guide to learning Rashi.

Nachman Bulman

Rabbi Nachman Bulman

137/21 Ma'alot Daphna, Jerusalem 97762 Israel •Tel: 02-824321 :טל' • 97762 ירושלים 137\21 מעלות דפנה

Dedication

זכרון נצח לאבינו

ר׳ שלמה יהודא ז״ל בן ר׳ אברהם ע״ה

נפטר ב׳ מרחשון תשמ״ט

איש אמת וישר, תמים בדרכיו

אהוב ומרוצה לכל יודעיו ומכיריו

זכרון נצח לאמנו

מרת אסתר מלכה ז״ל בת שרגא פיבל ע״ה

נפטרה א׳ דראש חודש אדר ב׳ תשנ״ז

חכמת נשים בנתה ביתה

מסרה נפשה לגדל ולחנך בניה ובתה

ענוה, טובת לב ויראת שמים היתה

צאצאיהם למשפחות מילר ושמידמן

In Honor of our Mother

Mrs. Evelyn Zuckerman, שתחיה.

A woman of valor who continues to
toil for Jewish causes and Torah values.

and

In Memory of our Parents

Mr. Philip Zuckerman   ר׳ פסח יהודה ב״ר יצחק אייזיק ז״ל

Mr. Israel Ray   ר׳ ישראל צבי ב״ר ברוך ז״ל

Mrs. Shaindel Ray   האשה שיינדל בת ר׳ ישראל ע״ה

Whose lives were dedicated to Torah
and the furtherance of Jewish education.

Their children

Howard and Rosalyn Zuckerman

— CONTENTS —

Acknowledgements

Torah study in America is flourishing. It wasn't always so. The seeds of Torah study, transplanted from Europe in the beginning of the century, only began to take root by the year 1940. It was then that Torah education began its spectacular climb, transforming America's nearly barren wilderness into the vibrant, productive Torah institutions and communities of today. It was in those difficult war years, while Hitler satanically and systematically destroyed European Jewry, that American Jewry built the foundations of Torah education in earnest. The seeds of traditional Torah study and lifestyle were planted and watered by the dedication of American-born men, themselves often deprived of a full Torah education. They made it their lifetime passion and pursuit to guarantee that their children would not be so deprived. It was an exciting time in American Jewish history. Unpretentious men, *balei batim*, many unfamiliar with the pathways of Torah study, they were nonetheless men of clear vision, courage and personal sacrifice. They were driven individuals. Frequently their personal needs for economic survival took second place, as they enthusiastically plowed their energies into turning arid America into fertile ground for Torah living. I was one of the early beneficiaries of their efforts.

It is with this acknowledgement in the foreground that I publish this modest contribution to Torah study for American, English-speaking students. The Torah pioneers of that era are the inspiration for this work. One of those pioneers was my father, Sam Bonchek, ע"ה. His selfless dedication and joyous sense of humor made him known and beloved among his fellow builders of Torah institutions. His partner, my mother, was not just a companion, but a skilled associate, who shared equally in this work. They were among the dedicated founders, over fifty years ago, of the Hebrew Academy of Cleveland, today a leader in pedagogical methods of Torah education.

Among my teachers, it is most fitting to acknowledge my first teacher of Chumash and Rashi. She was Rebbetzin Sarah Machlis, ע"ה, who taught at the Hebrew Academy. Her image is indelibly inscribed in my memory. Over half a century has passed since she taught us the famous Rashi of *parshas Noah*. "Some learn this as praise and some as deprecation . . ." and to this day I can still remember that classroom scene.

Also at the Academy in those years was Rabbi Meyer Zanitzky, שליט"א, who has given me many insights into Rashi over the years. I am thankful for the years of friendship we have shared, albeit at a distance.

Over the years my other Rebbeim at Telshe Yeshiva (Cleveland), the Bais

— ix

Midrash L'Torah (Chicago) and Ner Yisrael of Baltimore have imparted to me both a love of learning and an appreciation of its depth and breadth.

While I acknowledge these teachers' contribution to my education, they certainly are not to be held accountable for the quality of this work. I would be proud for them to share in any praise it may receive, but any criticism must be borne by me alone.

My *chavrusa*, Rabbi Yitzchak Frank (author of *The Practical Talmud Dictionary* and *Grammar for Gemara*) has given me some very helpful advice during the preparation of this book, and several of his ideas have been incorporated into its organization. My grateful thanks to him.

My most loving critic is my wife Shulamis. I thank her for reading and rereading this manuscript and for making many corrections and helpful suggestions. The title for this book was her idea. No words can fully express my gratitude for her consideration and thoughtfulness; they constantly remind me how fortunate I am. May Hashem grant her much nachas from the fruits of her work, our wonderful family.

My cousins and publishers, Elcya and Avi Weiss, of Laser Pages, have shown unlimited patience in helping prepare the manuscript. Their professionalism, and sincere concern and desire to help me produce a reader-friendly book not only made the publication possible but also eased the birth pangs of this endeavor. Many thanks to them. Special words of praise to Ruthie Fuld, of Laser Pages, for her artful sense of graphics, which gave these pages their tasteful appeal. Batsheva Aryeh, also of Laser Pages, did meticulous work in the final work-up, for which I am grateful. Marcy Tabak, of Feldheim Publishers, graciously offered me helpful advice on several important issues.

My deepest appreciation to the Creator for giving me the interest, ability and opportunity to produce this work on Rashi. May my efforts redound to the glory of His Torah.

APPRECIATING RASHI

The study of Rashi is a discipline. Like all disciplines, it has its rules. Like all disciplines, it requires effort. And like all disciplines, there is great satisfaction in mastering it.

Rashi's commentary on the Torah is highly praised and has been recognized as the Torah commentary par excellence ever since it was written over 900 years ago. The passing generations have not diminished appreciation for Rashi. On the contrary, the respect, one could even say, the love, for Rashi's work has grown with time. Today, every Torah student knows of Rashi's fame; he is taught to respect him while he is taught the commentary itself.

Yet hand-me-down respect is not the same as the hard, earned appreciation that one acquires from personally grappling with Rashi's ideas and discovering their brilliance through one's own efforts. This is one of the benefits to be gained from learning the discipline of Rashi.

This alone would make the effort worthwhile. But there are other benefits as well. An analogy should make my point clear. Learning Rashi without an in-depth understanding of his approach is like eating an apple and throwing away the seeds. One has momentary satisfaction, but, because one hasn't penetrated to the "core" of Rashi's idea, the student cannot make use of this knowledge to cultivate future fruits. By plumbing the depths of Rashi's commentary, getting into his mental shoes, so to speak, one learns an approach to Torah interpretation which can be applied throughout the Tanach. And in addition to all this, there comes an immensely enhanced appreciation for the wisdom of the Torah.

RASHI AND P'SHAT INTERPRETATION

Rashi is known as a commentator who focuses on *p'shat*, the plain sense of the text, as opposed to *drash*, explanation, or *sod*, the mystical interpretation. Early on in his Torah commentary he makes us aware of this by his well-known caveat, "I have come only to explain the plain sense of the Scripture (*p'shuto shel Mikra*)" (Rashi, Genesis 3:8).

Does Rashi mean that *all* of his Torah commentary is *p'shat* and never anything else? The question has been debated by the major super-commentaries on Rashi. The issue is a complex one and is further complicated by differing definitions of the concept of *p'shat*. We cannot go into the finer points of this matter here. Suffice it to say that one difficulty with the opinion that *all* of Rashi's comments are geared to *p'shat*, is that many times we find midrashim in Rashi that can be construed as *p'shat* only by stretching the imagination greatly. On the other hand, there are certainly instances when Rashi's use of midrashim gives us a clearer understanding of *p'shat*.

Everything considered, it is the better part of wisdom to assume that if Rashi cites a midrash, it is because his keen eye has noticed some problem in the text which makes understanding *p'shat* difficult. The midrash is intended to solve it. By closely analyzing these Rashi comments, we become sensitive to subtle difficulties in the Torah text itself — difficulties that, without Rashi's comment, we would have passed over without a second thought. The heightened awareness gained in this way is an important advantage in attaining a fuller and deeper understanding of the *p'shat*. We will see many examples of this in this book.

THE PURPOSES OF RASHI'S COMMENTARY ON THE TORAH

When we compare Rashi's Torah commentary with his magnum opus, the commentary on the Talmud, we can better see the unique aspects of his Torah work. The Talmudic one is a running commentary; it leads the student along the way, parallel to the Talmudic arguments. It offers him a step-by-step explanation at crucial junctures, in order to enable him to follow the complex Talmudic discourse smoothly and thereby avoid potential misunderstandings. Rashi's Torah commentary, on the other hand, has a different agenda. In a general sense, we could say that he strives to give the student a greater appreciation of the literal meaning and spiritual message of the Torah text. More specifically, we can identify several separate purposes of his Torah commentary.

- Resolving various types of difficulties in the text. This includes translating unfamiliar words into more familiar Hebrew words or into Old French, and explaining grammatical oddities.

- Clarifying questions that arise from apparent contradictions, puzzling non sequiturs or unclear passages in the Torah text.

- Elucidating the implications of Jewish law as derived from the text.

- Negating likely misunderstandings in the text and replacing them with more correct interpretations.

- Inspiring the student by means of midrashic teachings related to the text.

RASHI'S STYLE

In and of themselves these goals are not particulary unique for a Torah commentator. What is unique about Rashi's work is his inimitable style. In the 900 years since Rashi forged the way for Torah exegesis, no one has equalled his singularly brilliant method of interpretation.

His commentary sparkles with brevity, clarity and fine-tuned precision. It is not only what he says, but how he says it, that conveys a maximum of meaning in a minimum of words. This bespeaks a craftsman's artistry.

There are three characteristics of Rashi's commentary style which we must constantly bear in mind in attempting to understand what he says. His commentary is:

1. Based almost exclusively on the Torah text. Although this is not always obvious, it is nearly always true. This requires the student to search closely the words of the Torah to uncover what Rashi is relating to. Rashi never "just" comments. *Something about the text impels him to comment.*

2. Simple and straightforward. The comment is rarely complex, though the student may have to engage in complex thinking in order to arrive at Rashi's straightforward meaning. It is profoundly simple and simply profound. We must divest our thinking of gratuitous intricacies and train our minds to think simply and clearly in order to fully understand his meaning. Once we do, seemingly mind-stumping questions evaporate effortlessly.

3. Brief and precise in its choice of words. The student's respect for Rashi only begins when he internalizes this point. We can only arrive at the full meaning of Rashi's comments if we take his every word and its particular grammatical construction with the utmost seriousness. Confusion and misunderstanding arise when we casually gloss over his choice of words and the particular way he puts them together.

Some Keys to Understanding Rashi's Commentary

While much can be said about how Rashi approaches the task of commentary, I will limit myself to several basic points.

First and foremost, Rashi's commentary is built on a "question and answer" principle. The commentary is meant to answer questions that arise from the text. While this may be true for all commentary, Rashi's presents us with a particular problem. He never — or hardly ever — tells us what the question is! Every Rashi comment is an answer to a question. What is the question? *That* is the question!

Discovering the implicit question behind Rashi's comment is what the study of Rashi is all about. Finding out "What is bothering Rashi" is the stuff of Rashi interpretation. Rashi's commentary on the Chumash has spawned a prodigious literature. Well over one hundred and fifty Torah scholars are known to have written *their* commentary on Rashi's! That startling fact alone gives us some idea of the vibrant intellectual challenge that studying Rashi presents. Common to most of these super-commentaries is the task of suggesting what problem in the Torah text lead Rashi to comment — the comment being, in effect, his answer to this unstated question.

Two Types of Rashi Comments

For centuries both Ashkenazi and Sephardi teachers have taught their young pupils to critically analyze Rashi's comments by asking one of two possible questions, depending on the type of comment Rashi makes. I call them TYPE I and TYPE II comments.

Type I Comment

When a sentence in the Torah presents a difficulty in understanding, such as contradictions, unclarities or non sequiturs, then Rashi comes to supply an answer to the difficulty, without telling us what the difficulty is. In this case we should ask: "What in the text is bothering Rashi?" Most Rashi comments fall into this category. We will see that even midrashic comments frequently have their impetus in some problem in the text that is "bothering Rashi."

An example will help clarify this.

Genesis 24:62

ויצחק בא מבוא באר לחי ראי וגו׳

Rashi comments here:

מבוא באר לחי ראי: שהלך להביא הגר לאברהם אביו שישאנה.
Just come from the well Lachai Roi: *Rashi:* For he had gone to bring Hagar (back) to Abraham his father that he might take her (again) as his wife.

Here Rashi cites a midrash. Why? We must assume that there is some difficulty in the text. We ask: What is bothering Rashi here?

Our answer: The words בא מבוא which literally mean, "came from coming," are strangely redundant. The word מבוא is awkward and unnecessary. It should have said simply, "And Isaac came from the well . . ." The apparently redundant and unusual word מבוא is probably what is bothering Rashi. Therefore, Rashi tells us that the word is not redundant, it has a special message. Here the word מבוא has the sense of "bringing" (להביא in Rashi's comment) and not "coming" as we might have thought. What was Isaac bringing? Why Hagar, of course, because she was last seen at this very same well of Lachai Roi (see Genesis 16:14) and she is next seen as being Abraham's next wife (see Genesis 25:1 and Rashi's comment there).

We now see how Rashi's comment answers this difficulty. And Rashi has done so in his inimitable way, by teaching us a moral lesson. Note the special beauty in this comment: Isaac was engaged in finding a mate for his father (after Sarah's death), just as Abraham was engaged in finding a mate for his son. The Torah wants to convey to us the beauty of the reciprocal concern and love between father and son.

TYPE II COMMENT

When the Torah sentence is likely to be misunderstood, Rashi will add a word or two of clarification to guide the student around the error and the right direction. The appropriate question for the student to ask here is: "What misunderstanding is Rashi warning us about and helping us avoid?" How would I have (mis)understood the Torah's words had Rashi not commented? These comments have an identifying style. They usually consist of a few words that Rashi inserts or adds to the words of the Torah. Rashi will either paraphrase the Torah's words or he will quote them, as he makes slight emendations. This is a less-frequent type of comment, though it appears often enough.

Let's see an example of this.

Genesis 30:35

"וַיָּסַר בַּיּוֹם הַהוּא אֶת הַתְּיָשִׁים הָעֲקֻדִּים וְהַטְּלֻאִים וְגוֹ' . . . ".

וַיָּסַר: לָבָן בַּיּוֹם הַהוּא.

He removed: *Rashi:* Laban on that day.

Here is a typical Type II comment. Notice Rashi adds only the word "Laban" and inserts it into the words of the Torah. Rashi's intent is clear: he wants to tell us that it was Laban — and not Jacob — who removed the spotted he-goats from the flock. This is necessary because from the words of the Torah — "And he removed, etc." — it is not clear who did the removing.

Actually, without Rashi's clarification, I would have assumed that it was Jacob who removed the goats. I would have done so because a few sentences earlier it is Jacob who says: "I will pass through all thy flock today, removing from there every one of the flock, etc" (Genesis 30:32).

Nevertheless, Rashi tells us that it was not Jacob who did the removing of the sheep.

We must now ask: How did Rashi know that in fact it was Laban and not Jacob? A fuller look at this section will show us how Rashi came to his judgement. Sentence 36 removes all doubt about the matter, for it says: "And he set three days' journey between himself (i.e., Laban) and Jacob, etc." The "he" here refers to Laban and thus the previous sentence must also refer to Laban.

You can readily see that here we wouldn't ask: "What is bothering Rashi?" because there is nothing really problematic in the text. We would rather ask,

"What misunderstanding of the text is Rashi helping us avoid?"

I call these two types of comments: Type I and Type II comments. Usually, when we first approach a Rashi comment, we don't know which type it is, nor can we be certain at the outset what in the text prompted it. But, as I mentioned, the two types frequently have different styles and this can serve as a hint as to what is the basis in the text. Of course these are not hard and fast categories; many Rashi comments seem to be a combination of both types, and some may be neither! But as a rule of thumb the categorization should help the student probe the deeper meaning of Rashi's commentary.

The student should keep the two types of comments in mind as he studies Rashi; they are basic tools of interpreting his commentary. Using them correctly is much more difficult than may appear at first glance, but the effort pays off in a better understanding of Rashi.

The Levels of Understanding Rashi

One of the early Rashi commentators, Rav Avraham Bakrat (end of the fifteenth century), has pointed out in his *Sefer Zikaron* that the process of understanding Rashi consists of three stages or levels. They are:

1. Understanding *what* he says; knowing what each word means and the basic point of his comment.

2. Understanding *why* he feels the necessity to comment — what in the text prompted it. (The Type I and Type II questions mentioned above.)

3. Understanding *what support* there is for Rashi's interpretation.

These three steps are, in effect, the different levels of appreciating Rashi. Many students read Rashi's comment and are satisfied when they know WHAT he said. Correct understanding of *what* his comment says is obviously essential to comprehending it, but this is only the first step in understanding.

More advanced students realize that Rashi may be answering a question that is as yet unclear to them. They may reflexively search the Rashi commentaries, the most popular being the *Sifsei Chachomim*, to see what they suggest may be Rashi's unstated question. But when the student strives to discover Rashi's question *on his own*, without the help of the supercommentaries, it is then that he is truly engaged in the study of Rashi. This can be called the first level of *in-depth* understanding.

There is yet a deeper level of Rashi interpretation which is less often appreciated. This is Bakrat's third stage, which entails searching the Torah text to find support for, and thus validation of, Rashi's interpretation. Since every interpretation is indirectly a rejection of other possible interpretations, we must always ask: What evidence is there that Rashi's interpretation is correct? Disputes between Rashi and the Ramban, for example, are golden opportunities to see how each approaches the Torah's words and structure and arrive at their own individual *p'shat* interpretations. When we study these commentaries closely, we see that their interpretations are not arbitrary inventions, but rather that they always have their support in the Torah text.

An EXAMPLE OF THREE-LEVEL DEPTH INTERPRETATION

To make this discussion less abstract, let us look at an example from Genesis 2:9.

Here is a brief and simple Rashi comment, yet it too has to be closely examined. We must ask: Why the need for the comment?

Genesis 2:9

ויצמח ה׳ אלוקים מן האדמה כל עץ נחמד למראה וטוב למאכל
ועץ החיים בתוף הגן ועץ הדעת טוב ורע.

בתוך הגן: באמצע . . .

In the midst of the garden: *Rashi:* In the middle.

First-Level Interpretation:

What is Rashi saying?

On the face of it, it seems quite obvious what Rashi is saying. He is telling us that the words בתוך הגן mean "in the middle of the garden." But then, this is *so* obvious that we wonder why he even has to make the point. The first level of understanding must get us past this question. Our answer here is that in actuality the words בתוך הגן could have two possible translations. They could mean

1. "in the middle" or
2. "in the midst."

These are by no means identical terms. The first tells us that the Tree was right in the middle of the garden, while the second choice only means that the Tree was somewhere *inside* the Garden. It is not immediately clear which of these two interpretations is the correct one.

Second-Level Interpretation:

Why does Rashi feel it necessary to make this comment?

Our answer here is that if the word בתוך means in the midst (i.e., inside) of the garden, then there's no reason for the Torah to add this word; it could just say that the Tree was בגן ("in the garden") and we would know that the Tree was "in the (midst of the) garden." On the other hand, if the word בתוך means "in the middle" of the garden, then the word is significant, for it tells us not only that the Tree was in the garden, but also its exact location there — "in the middle of the garden". Rashi's brief explanation tells us that the word בתוך is not superfluous — it informs us as to the specific place. This is Rashi's message with his one-word comment — באמצע.

Third-Level Interpretation:

What support is there for Rashi's comment?

We look for supportive evidence for Rashi's interpretation from somewhere else in the story or somewhere else in the Torah.

In this case if we look at chapter 3, we can find support for Rashi's *p'shat*. See, sentences 1-3.

1. והנחש היה ערום מכל חית השדה אשר עשה ה' אלוקים ויאמר אל האשה אף כי אמר אלוקים לא תאכלו מכל עץ הגן . . .
2. ותאמר האשה אל הנחש מפרי עץ הגן נאכל . . .
3. ומפרי העץ אשר בתוך הגן אמר אלוקים לא תאכלו ממנו ולא תגעו בו, פן תמותון.

1. Now the serpent was more subtle than any animal of the field which the L-rd G-d had made. And it said to the woman: Although G-d has said, You shall not eat of every tree of the Garden . . .
2. And the woman said to the serpent, We may eat of the fruit of the trees of the garden . . .
3. But of the fruit of the tree which is בתוך the garden, G-d has said, You shall not eat of it neither shall you touch it . . ."

This should clarify the matter. Certainly in this verse the word בתוך must mean "in the middle," for if it meant "in the midst (i.e., inside) of the garden" this designation wouldn't differentiate the Tree of Knowledge from the other trees; they were *all* inside the garden.

On this basis, it would seem, Rashi concluded that in our verse the word בתוך must likewise mean "in the middle" and not "in the midst." We have found support for Rashi's interpretation, thus satisfying the third level of in-depth interpretation.

I have intentionally chosen a simple Rashi comment in order to illustrate the idea of a three-level analysis. But we will come across more complicated Rashi interpretations, where finding support for his *p'shat* is crucial, since he may take an opposing view to that of the Ramban, Ibn Ezra or other commentators.

Note also that this comment is a very brief one, just one word. This is characteristic of a Type II comment; it is meant to guide the student gently around a possible misunderstanding: that the word בתוך means "in the midst."

Here we have the three levels of analysis: What Rashi says, why he says it and the textual evidence supporting his interpretation. If we want to fully appreciate Rashi, we must be able to understand how he would defend himself against alternative interpretations. Applying these three levels of analysis gives us entry into the deeper recesses of Rashi's mind. We can see how a simple Rashi comment presents us with a challenge to gain a fuller understanding of Rashi and consequently of the Torah itself. Following and fathoming the three levels of Rashi interpretation is the sum of understanding him in depth.

It should be clear from all this that studying Rashi in depth is not for the fainthearted. It requires a serious investment of mental energies, a basic knowledge of the text and much patience and perserverence.

TEXTS OF RASHI EDITIONS

When you open up a Chumash and read Rashi's commentary, are you reading what Rashi actually wrote? Have changes or copyists' errors crept into the text that we have in front of us today?

This is not an academic question, like asking whether Shakespeare or someone else wrote Hamlet. Knowing whether the words in any particular Rashi comment are Rashi's own words or not is a very practical matter. Since serious study of Rashi is heavily dependent on a close analysis of his every word, then it is of primary importance to know that the words we are analyzing are Rashi's own words. From Rashi's commentary on the Talmud we know of his obsession with precise wording and his economy of language. We have confidence that he was precise in his choice of words, but if the words we are studying are not his but just an error in recording, we would be wasting our time trying to interpret them. Our interpretations, however brilliant, would be fanciful explanations of something Rashi never wrote!

But, after 900 years, how can we be sure that each and every one of the printed Rashi comments we find in our Chumashim is, in fact, his original comment? Corruptions may have infiltrated the text. Rashi wrote some 400 years before the printing press was invented, so for hundreds of years all copies of his commentary were made by hand. Scribal errors were bound to enter into these later copies.

Once the printing press was invented in 1455, the Jews were among its most enthusiastic users. Only fifteen years after its invention, Jews began publishing printed Torah books. The very first Hebrew book printed was the Torah with Rashi's commentary! But printers too make errors — and printed errors multiply the effect of human error thousands of times over.

Some scholars have taken upon themselves the task of identifying the correct text of Rashi's Torah commentary. This involves comparing various early printed texts along with ancient Rashi manuscripts that have survived the generations, weighing the pros and cons of each difference and making an educated guess as to which of the different versions of a particular comment is the authentic one. Each Rashi comment has to be judged individually.

The average student has neither the time nor the knowledge to make such judgements. He needn't, for he can rely on such well-researched Rashi texts as Rabbi C. D. Chavel's Hebrew edition (published by Mossad Harav Kook) or the Rosenbaum and Silbermann annotated Rashi edition, in Hebrew and English (published by Feldheim). Once the student has a "feel" for Rashi's style, he can sometimes venture his own guess as to the most reasonable text. As an example of this kind of work, see our analysis of Genesis 45:28 in *parshas Vayigash.*

Knowing Rashi — Understanding Rashi

Knowing and understanding Rashi's Torah commentary are two, very different matters. One can *know* what Rashi says by reading his commentary. One can *know* what is bothering Rashi by reading one of the super-commentaries, such as the *Mizrachi*, the *Gur Aryeh* or the *Sifsei Chachomim*. But the student only begins to *understand* Rashi when he starts to *think* on his own. With the instant information highways of today, thinking on one's own has become a neglected art. But the study of Torah, in all its variations, including the study of Rashi, should be a very personal experience. If the question that bothered Rashi does not bother you, his answer will not excite you. If the Torah is read like a fact sheet, by absorbing information without questioning it, without the student's personal involvement, then the student has, at best, gained in knowledge but not in understanding. He has missed an opportunity to appreciate the wisdom of the Torah. Rashi's commentary, as I hope to show, is an excellent educational method for learning how to *understand* the Torah. But we must first understand Rashi!

How to Use This Book

The purpose of this book is to give the student a method, together with useful tools for understanding Rashi's Torah commentary. This book is intended to be, and is formulated as, a *workbook.* The student is asked to answer questions in writing. In this way he is encouraged to clarify his thoughts and to match them up with Rashi's thoughts.

By searching for the questions that Rashi is addressing and searching for answers to these questions, we activate our minds. In the process we begin to train ourselves to think as Rashi did.

This interactional approach is grounded in the assumption that learning takes root once we begin to ask questions. Our understanding improves as we learn to ask more relevant questions. The Talmudic method of clarifying concepts through questions and answers is most appropriate here. Therefore, to the extent that the reader takes the time to write down his questions and his answers to the questions posed in this book, his understanding will grow.

THE BOOK'S ORGANIZATION

The book is divided into the *parshiyos hashavua* of the book of Bereishis (Genesis.) In each *parshah*, three or four Rashi comments are analyzed. Each comment is organized in a way that I hope will help the student learn to analyze Rashi's meaning. After the Torah verse is presented, Rashi's comment is quoted (on a grey background) in Hebrew and in English. I then divide the analysis into several parts.

The first part I call, **"Questioning Rashi."** Here the student is asked to critically examine the comment and ask himself any one of a number of possible questions, such as:

Why is it necessary? Our premise is: Rashi does not comment unless he feels the need to clarify something. If Rashi quotes a midrash, it is always appropriate to ask: Why the need for the midrash?

If it looks like a Type II comment (short, inserted within the words of the verse), we could ask: What misunderstanding is likely here?

The second part I call **"What Is Bothering Rashi?"** Here, the student is asked to figure out what in the Torah verse or larger context presents a difficulty that Rashi is addressing.

The next part is called **"Understanding Rashi."** Here, we see how Rashi's comment is meant to answer the assumed difficulty in the text.

Then, when appropriate, I have a section called **"Support for Rashi's Interpretation."** The student is asked to search out the Torah section and see if he can find additional support for the way Rashi interprets the verse.

Sometimes there are additional sections, intended to help the student get a deeper look at the comment or a closer look at the subtleties in Rashi's wording.

THE DIBBUR HAMASCHIL

All Rashi comments begin with a *dibbur hamaschil* "lead words," the words quoted from the Torah which form the basis for his comment. The *dibbur hamaschil* play an important part in understanding Rash's intent. Some supercommentaries claim that all Rashi comments are aimed exclusively at explaining the *dibbur hamaschil*, while most feel that while this is usually true, it is not an inflexible rule. We will see many examples where examining the *dibbur hamaschil* closely helps us better understand the Rashi comment.

SOURCES

A word about the sources used in researching this book. The commentators on Rashi, Rishonim and Acharonim devoted their efforts to interpreting what his comments mean, what difficulties in the text prompted them and what support there is for them. I have made use of many such super-commentaries. Many Rashi comments were analyzed with the help of more than one commentator. It would be difficult and confusing to cite at every turn in the analysis the different commentary used. Instead I have chosen the path of the author of the famous Tanach commentary *Metzudas Dovid*. He writes the following at the end of his classic work:

> Since it was virtually impossible to mention in each place from whose womb what went forth and who begat it, I find myself obligated to list here the names of the commentators from whom I gathered and refined this commentary. This should be considered as if I specified them throughout [my commentary].

I too will mention those super-commentaries whose wisdom I made use of:

Amer Nakeh of Rav Ovadia Bartinuro; Be'er BaSadeh; Be'er Mayim Chayim; Be'er Yitzchak; Da'as Zekeinim MiBalei HaTosaphos; Devek Tov; Divrei Dovid; Divrei Negidim; Gur Aryeh (Maharal); Havanas HaMikra (Heidenheim, Wolf); Heichal Rashi; Ibn Ezra, Avraham; Levush HaOrah; L'Pshuto shel Rashi; Lubavitcher Rebbe, (Reb Menachem Mendel Schneerson, Be'urim L'Perush Rashi); Maharasha; Maskil L'Dovid; Mesiach Illmim; Minchas Yehudah; Mizrachi, Eliyahu; Nachalas Ya'akov; Ohr HaChayim; Parshandasah; Pentateuch with Rashi (Rosenbaum & Silbermann); Perushei Rashi, Chavel (Mossad HaRav Kook), Rashbam; Rashi al HaTorah (Berliner); Rashi HaShalem (Ariel); Rashi on the Torah, Saperstein Edition (Artscroll); Sefer Zikaron; Sifsei Chachomim; Ramban; Tiferes Yosef; Tzeida LaDerech; Yosef Hallel.

For the student who wants to delve deeper on his own, I cite, at the end of each analysis, those super-commentaries who formed the main basis for my analysis of the Rashi comment. It should be understood that the commentaries on Rashi frequently offer different approaches to any one comment. I have used my judgement in choosing those that seem to best explain the comment. But certainly there are other possible interpretations. One of the purposes of this book is to help the student begin to use his own analytical skills to decipher Rashi. I would be untrue to this goal if I, myself, did not ultimately rely on my judgement in interpreting Rashi. At the same time, I am fully aware that my judgement is limited. The study of Torah thrives on the interchange of different opinions. It is the give and take that results from various opinions in Torah study that has been called *l'hagdil Torah U'lehadirah* —"to make Torah great and to glorify it." I would be quite happy — actually, excited — if the book leads to "conversations" about the best way to understand Rashi.

I end this introduction with my best wishes for the student's success as he enters this exciting, enlightening and inspiring endeavor of learning Chumash with Rashi.

The study of Rashi is a discipline.

Sit down at Rashi's feet, . . . and allow yourself
to become his disciple.

The following Rashi comment is an excellent example of the subtleties in Rashi. Understanding the reason for his comment makes us aware of nuances in the Torah text itself which we might otherwise have overlooked.

Let us analyze the comment step by step.

Genesis 1:4

וירא אלוקים את האור כי טוב ויבדל אלוקים בין האור ובין החשך.

וירא אלוקים את האור כי טוב ויבדל: אף בזה אנו צריכים לדברי אגדה, ראהו שאינו כדאי להשתמש בו רשעים והבדילו לצדיקים לעתיד לבא. ולפי פשוטו כך פרשהו: ראהו כי טוב ואין נאה לו ולחושך שיהיו משתמשים בערבוביא, וקבע לזה תחומו ביום ולזה תחומו בלילה.

And G-d saw that the light was good and He separated: *Rashi:* Here too we need the words of the Aggadah: He saw that the wicked were unworthy of using it; He therefore set it apart (ויבדל) for the righteous in the World to Come. But according to its plain sense (פשוטו) explain it thus: He saw that it was good and that it was not seemly that the light and darkness should function together in a confused manner. He therefore limited this one's sphere of activity to the daytime and this one's sphere of activity to the nighttime.

Questioning Rashi

Our first task is to question Rashi. The first question on a Rashi comment is usually: What is bothering Rashi? That is to say, what in the text is unusual or problematic which prompts Rashi to make his comment? To discover the answer to that question you begin by asking your own questions on Rashi's comment. Write down any questions you can think of on this comment.

Your Questions:

Questions: 1. What difficulty does this comment come to answer?
2. Why did Rashi believe that "here too we need the words of the Aggadah"? Why use an Aggadah to explain the verse? Remember Rashi's preference for *p'shat.*
3. Once Rashi has given us his first interpretation, why did he need to offer the *p'shat* interpretation?
4. And finally, why is the Aggadah brought first before the *p'shat?* One would think that the first order of business would be a *p'shat* interpretation.

To go about answering these questions you must carefully study

the *dibbur hamaschil,* "lead words,"

the comment itself, and

the sentence on which the comment is based.

What Is Bothering Rashi? _____

Can you find what is bothering Rashi?

Your Answer:

Do you need a hint?

Hint #1:

Look at the *dibbur hamaschil.* What is strange about Rashi's choice of words here? Look at the Torah text itself. Can you see what is unusual about the combination of words that Rashi has chosen? Understanding this should help you understand what is bothering Rashi.

Think...

Your Answer:

An Answer: If you looked carefully you certainly noticed that Rashi joins the word ויבדל with the first part of the sentence. But in fact this word comes after the *esnachta* (comma) and thus should really be separated from the previous words. Why then does Rashi join the two parts of the sentence?

Think! . . .

YOUR ANSWER:

If you haven't gotten it yet, here's another hint.

> *Hint #2:*
>
> Look at the words in the Torah which Rashi quotes and compare them to the parallel phrases found throughout this chapter. Take, for example, the following: "And G-d called the dry land Earth and the gathering of the waters he called Seas; and G-d saw that it was good" (1:10).
>
> See also 1:12, 1:18, 1:21, 1:25. What is the difference between the phrase here and the others? Can you point out the difference that Rashi seems to be sensitive to?

YOUR ANSWER:

An Answer: Elsewhere in the Creation story, wherever it says "And G-d saw that it was good" it doesn't specify what G-d saw that was good. Here it does, for it says, "And G-d saw the light that it was good." This difference calls for an explanation.

The second peculiarity with this sentence is that all the other times when it says "And G-d saw it was good" the phrase comes at the end of a sentence, a final statement with nothing following. But here this phrase has a second half to it, "and He separated etc." This also puzzles Rashi. What does the Torah want to tell us by putting the first statement ("And G-d saw the light, that it was good . . .") together with the second half of the sentence ("and He separated between the light and the darkness")? When a sentence is made up of two parts there is always some conceptual or causal connection between the first part and the second part.

Rashi is bothered by these peculiarities. How does his Aggadic interpretation deal with this?

Think . . .

YOUR ANSWER:

Understanding Rashi

Because of these peculiarities Rashi concludes two things:

    1) Seeing that the light was good is particularly significant, and
    2) Seeing that the light was good is in some way connected with the

15 —

fact that G-d separated the light from the darkness (since they are paired together in the same sentence). The question is: In what way is the "goodness" of the light related to the fact that it was separated and set apart by itself?

The Aggadah serves to suggest a way in which the two parts might be connected: The fact that G-d saw that the light was good caused Him to make a separation and save it exclusively for the righteous. The "seeing that it was good" led to "and He separated."

A Deeper Look

The midrash which Rashi quotes derives this idea (that the light was set aside for the righteous) in a way which is most characteristic of midrashic interpretations — by means of word association. (See Psalms 97:11: "The light is sown for the righteous, etc.") We see that the righteous can look forward to harvesting the light. Note also Isaiah 3:10: "Say for the righteous כי טוב it is good." We find the same words, "it is good," in Genesis as a definition of the light and in Isaiah as a definition of the righteous! So the idea that Light will be saved (harvested) for the righteous at some later date has its roots in various prophetic utterances.

Rashi's P'shat Explanation

We have discussed Rashi's Aggadic interpretation. Now, how does his *p'shat* interpretation deal with the matter of connecting the two parts of the sentence?

Your Answer:

An Answer: Rashi's *p'shat* explanation also shows how the two parts of the sentence are connected. Because G-d "saw that it [the light] was good," He realized it was not fitting that the light should be mixed together (diluted) with the darkness and therefore, "He separated...light from darkness."

We now understand what bothered Rashi, how he dealt with the difficulties, and why his *dibbur hamaschil* connected "and He separated" with the first part of the sentence. But we must still understand why he offered the Aggadic explanation *before* the *p'shat*, even though generally *p'shat* is preferred.

Can you think of a reason?

YOUR ANSWER:

An Answer: I would say that Rashi gives us the Aggadah first, even though he
usually favors *p'shat*, because he had used Aggadic interpretations
in the previous sentences. He thus continues with the Aggadic line
of thought. As he himself writes, "Here *too* we need the Aggadah...".
Only after he is finished with the Aggadah does he offer his *p'shat* interpretation.

FURTHER ANALYSIS

We haven't finished yet with a thorough analysis of this comment. Most
commentators agree that when Rashi offers two intepretations he does
so because each, individually, is somewhat deficient. In this case we
must understand what is "deficient" in the first that brings him to offer a
p'shat interpretation as well.

What would you say is lacking in the first interpretation?

YOUR ANSWER:

An Answer: I would suggest that since Rashi generally favors *p'shat*, he can't
be satisfied only with a *drash* interpretation if a *p'shat* one can be
found. Thus, he gives the *p'shat* as well.

Can you explain why Rashi considers only the second interpretation to be *p'shat*
but not the first?

Think . . .

YOUR ANSWER:

An Answer: The Aggadic interpretation speaks about the World to Come. This
is not characteristic of the Written Torah; otherwordly rewards are not
mentioned explicitly in the Torah on a *p'shat* level.

We now have understood what in the text bothered Rashi and how he answers the
difficulty both on an Aggadic and a *p'shat* level.

(See Gur Aryeh)

For those familiar with Rashi this comment is well known. Yet a close analysis of Rashi demands that we understand why a midrash is chosen in order to understand p'shat.

Genesis 2:18

ויאמר הי אלוקים לא טוב היות האדם לבדו אעשה לו עזר כנגדו.

לא טוב היות וגוי׳: שלא יאמרו שתי רשויות הן הקב״ה בעליונים
יחיד ואין לו זוג, וזה בתחתונים אין לו זוג.

It is not good that [man] should be, etc: *Rashi:* So that people may not say that there are two deities, the Holy One, blessed be He, the only One among the celestial beings without a mate, and this one (Adam) the only one among the terrestrial beings, without a mate.

QUESTIONING RASHI

Can you think of questions to ask on this comment?

YOUR QUESTIONS:

Here are some questions you should ask:

1. The meaning of this sentence appears self-evident. "It is not good for man to remain alone, so I must find him a wife." Why does Rashi feel the need to explain it? Remember, Rashi does not comment just for the sake of commenting; he comments only when the words of the Torah prompt him to explain some difficulty. In other words, what is bothering Rashi?
2. And why does he explain it with a midrash? How does this help our understanding of the text?

Do you have answers to these questions?

YOUR ANSWERS:

WHAT IS BOTHERING RASHI?

An Answer: A knowledge of Hebrew is necessary here. The choice of words in this sentence is somewhat unusual.

Clue:

Note the *dibbur hamaschil*. See the words that Rashi quotes and also note that he adds 'וגו, "etc." This means that we must pay attention first and foremost to the words he quotes, while bearing in mind the rest of the sentence, that is, the meaning of 'וגו. The addition of 'וגו tells us that Rashi doesn't quote all the words that are relevant to the difficulty. It means that the interpretation he will offer relates as well to the unquoted words.

Can you detect anything unusual or problematic with the words Rashi quotes?

YOUR ANSWER:

An Answer: The word היות is unusual in this context. The common rendering "to be" is incorrect; that would be להיות. The word היות means "being." Thus the correct translation is "It is not good, being that man is alone," and not "It is not good for man to be alone." With this corrected translation we can better understand Rashi's difficulty. For now the sentence reads: It is not [a] good [situation] being that man is alone. Rashi implicitly asks: What is it that is not good? How does his comment deal with this question?

YOUR ANSWER:

UNDERSTANDING RASHI

Rashi's comment answers this question. If man remains alone, without a mate, the impression will be given that man is a deity. And *that* is not good!

 See how Rashi uses a midrash. The midrash explains away a difficulty in the text in a way that is close to, if not strictly, *p'shat*. At the same time it teaches us a lesson in humility: man was not created singly in order to divest him of any pretentions of divinity.

(See *Gur Aryeh)*

Rashi's unusual reading, at first difficult to justify, finds evidence in the context.

Genesis 4:13

ויאמר קין אל ה׳ גדול עוני מנשוא.

גדול עוני מנשוא. בתמיה: אתה טואן עליונים ותחתונים ועוני אי אפשר לטעון.

Is my sin greater than can be borne (forgiven)? *Rashi:* בתמיה. [To be read as a] question. You bear the worlds above and below, and it is impossible for You to forgive my sin?

Rashi tells us that Cain's statement is to be read as a question. He then quotes a midrash which explains Cain's thinking.

What would you ask here?

YOUR QUESTION:

QUESTIONING RASHI

Rashi takes Cain's words as a question, but they lack the conventional sign used in the Bible to indicate a question, the ה׳ השאלה.

A Question: Why does Rashi assume this is a question? On what basis can he turn a statement into a question? Taking such license can lead to ruinous consequences. For example, what if we turned statements into questions in the Ten Commandments. It would sound like this: Thou shalt not murder? Thou shalt not commit adultery? Thou shalt not steal? That is certainly not what the Torah had in mind.

Why then does Rashi do it here?

What Is Bothering Rashi?

YOUR ANSWER:

WHAT IS BOTHERING RASHI?

An Answer: If this verse is a statement and Cain is expressing his anguish over his sin, then his next statement doesn't fit in. He goes on to say, "Behold You have banished me this day from the face of the earth and I must avoid Your presence and become a restless wanderer on earth. Anyone who meets me may kill me." This sounds like Cain is arguing with G-d's judgement. He exclaims the magnitude of the punishment, as if to say: The punishment is not fair! To understand the words, "My sin is too great to forgive," would mean that Cain is admitting the enormity of his sin. This doesn't fit with a plea of mercy. If Cain wanted mercy from G-d, we would expect him to try to minimize his sin, not maximize it. So Rashi is bothered by the juxtaposition of Cain's admitting his guilt (if we translate our phrase as "My sin is too great to forgive") with his plea for mercy.

How does Rashi's interpretation avoid this problem?

YOUR ANSWER:

UNDERSTANDING RASHI

An Answer: By turning this phrase into a question, Rashi eliminates the difficulty. Cain is asking, "Why can't You forgive me? You forgive the whole universe—why not me?

This brief comment tells us that although the usual biblical indication of a question (i.e., the ה׳ השאלה) is absent from this phrase, it is nevertheless a question. Cain is saying, "Is my sin too great [for You] to forgive?"

WHAT SUPPORT CAN YOU FIND FOR RASHI'S INTERPRETATION

Review the section for evidence for Rashi's interpretation.

YOUR ANSWER:

An Answer: See sentence 4:15 where G-d assents to Cain's plea. He agrees to protect him from predators. From G-d's response we can deduce what Cain was after. He was arguing with G-d to obtain leniency. He was not consenting to the Divine decree, nor was he admitting the enormity of his sin. Rather he was asking rhetorically, "Is my sin too great to forgive?"

A Closer Look at Rashi's Interpretation: Rashi vs. Ramban and Ibn Ezra

Note how Rashi translates each word here. He translates עוני as "sin" and not as "punishment." He also translates the word מנשוא as "to forgive" and not as "to bear (suffer)." Rashi's translations here are not to be taken for granted.

This interpretation of Rashi's is at odds with those of some of the major commentators. The Ramban says the verse means: "My sin is too great to be borne [forgiven]." A confession of guilt. Note that this is similar to Rashi, except that in Rashi's interpretation the phrase is a rhetorical question, while for the Ramban it is a statement of fact.

Rashi is also at odds with Ibn Ezra, who says the phrase means: "My punishment is too great to bear." Ibn Ezra translates the word עוני as "punishment" and the word מנשוא as "to suffer."

In conclusion, Rashi's one-word comment, בתמיה, is an original view of p'shat.

(See L'Pheshuto shel Rashi)

Here we have a Rashi comment familiar to many, yet deeper analysis reveals Rashi's concern for understanding the subtleties of the text.

Genesis 6:9

אלה תולדת נח נח איש צדיק תמים היה בדרתיו את האלוקים התהלך נח.

בדורותיו: יש מרבותינו דורשים אותו לשבח, כל שכן אלו היה בדור צדיקים היה צדיק יותר. ויש שדורשים אותו לגנאי, לפי דורו היה צדיק ואלו היה בדורו של אברהם לא היה נחשב לכלום.

In his generations: *Rashi:* Some of our Rabbis explain it to his credit (he was righteous even in his generation); certainly if he would have lived in a generation of righteous men he would have been even more righteous. Others, however, explain it to his discredit: in his generation he was considered righteous, but had he lived in the generation of Abraham he wouldn't have been considered much.

QUESTIONING RASHI

What question can you ask on this Rashi?

YOUR QUESTION:

Questions: We can suggest several. First, our by-now familiar question: What is bothering Rashi? What is unclear, problematic or redundant in this sentence that prompts Rashi's comment?

We can add an additional question. Why does Rashi cite two contradictory interpretations, one to Noah's credit and one to his discredit? Why not one?

Can you answer these questions?

YOUR ANSWER:

What Is Bothering Rashi?

It is always important to pay close attention to the *dibbur hamaschil.*

Is that word (בדורותיו) unclear, problematic or redundant?

Think!

Certainly the word is redundant. Noah was righteous in his generation! When else would or could he be righteous, if not in his own generation, when he lived?

Thus, Rashi's first concern: Why the need for this word?

But this word is problematic in another sense. Look at it — in the Hebrew.

What do you see?

YOUR ANSWER:

An Answer: The Problem? The word is in the plural! In his generations! Does a man live in more than one generation? This, then, is the second problem Rashi addresses. How does he deal with it?

YOUR ANSWER:

Understanding Rashi

Because the word is redundant, Rashi searches for an explanation. He brings a midrash focusing on the word "in his generations," which can mean either

1. "even in his generation" — he was righteous in spite of the corruption of his generation, or
2. "only in his generation" — he was righteous only relative to the corruption of his generation.

Thus the word "in his generations" is not redundant at all.

But why in the plural?

DO YOU HAVE AN ANSWER?

An Answer: Actually the first opinion that Rashi quotes claims that Noah was righteous not only in his generation, but certainly in other generations as well. That is, he would have been considered righteous even in other generations. This, then, is the reason for the plural form — it is as if he were righteous in several generations.

But the second opinion doesn't answer the use of the plural form, since it implies that Noah was righteous only in his own generation. So why bring it?

YOUR ANSWER:

In order to answer this question and the one we asked above (why are two opinions brought), think which of the two seems to you to make the most sense in the context.

Hint:

Read the surrounding descriptions of Noah.

YOUR ANSWER:

An Answer: I would say that the Torah itself seems to imply that Noah's righteousness was only relative to his times. To see this in a larger context, look at the last sentences in the previous Parshah (6:5-8). There we are told that Noah "found favor in G-d's eyes." Note that this comes on the tail of the description of the evilness of that generation. This implies a relative evaluation of Noah—namely, that he found favor because of the evilness of his generation. See also 7:1: "for you I have seen righteous before Me *in this generation.*" This seems to be clear evidence for the second interpretation in Rashi.

P'shat interpretations are built both on contextual and grammatical considerations. Rashi's first interpretation is based more on grammatical factors (the use of the plural) than on context; the second interpretation is grounded more on context than on grammar, for when we look at other sentences in this Parshah we see evidence for the second interpretation. The two opinions satisfy two different *p'shat* requirements, each in its own way. So Rashi brings both opinions.

A FURTHER NOTE

Many commentators on this Rashi say that the two opinions (for praise or for discredit) do not differ as to the objective degree of Noah's righteousness. Both realize his righteousness was less than that of Abraham and certainly more than that of his contemporaries. They argue only as to the reason the Torah makes a point of adding the words "in his generations."

(See Mesiach Ilmim)

The following Rashi comment shows us several things: how Rashi uses p'shat and drash, why he sometimes needs both and how drash relates to the text.

Genesis 8:7

וישלח את הערב ויצא יצוא ושוב עד יבשת המים מעל הארץ.

עד יבשת המים: פשוטו כמשמעו, אבל מדרש אגדה: מוכן היה העורב לשליחות אחרת בעצירת גשמים בימי אליהו שנאמר: והעורבים מביאים לו לחם ובשר (מ"א י"ז)

Until the waters were dried up: *Rashi:* The real sense of the verse is what it plainly implies כמשמעו – פשוטו but the Midrashic explanation is: The raven was kept in readiness for another errand during the time when the rain was withheld in the days of Elijah, as it is said (I Kings 17:6), "And the ravens brought him bread and meat."

Before getting into Rashi's comment itself, we should understand the sense of the midrash. The most obvious explanation of this drash is that both in the story of Elijah and in the story of Noah the raven plays a part. We have an association: Raven . . . raven. In one case the raven was to do a service for Noah; in the other case it was to serve Elijah.

QUESTIONING RASHI

Yet this is usually not enough to explain Rashi's inclusion of a midrash into his commentary. Since Rashi readily acknowledges the *p'shat* and then cites a midrashic comment, we should ask: Why the need for the drash?

What difficulty in the text is the midrash addressing?

What Is Bothering Rashi?

An Answer: The point here is quite subtle.

Note the *dibbur hamaschil*. Anything strange about them?

Compare these words with those later on in 8:14:

Genesis 8:7	Genesis 8:14
עד יבושת המים	יבשה הארץ
"until the waters dried up"	"the earth dried up"

What dried up, the *waters* or the *earth*?

Water can't dry up—water can only be wet; there is no dry water! Earth, on the other hand, can be either dry or wet. Yet in 8:7, it says the waters dried up! Notice that in 8:14, it says the earth (not the waters) dried up. Why the choice of such words here? Is this perhaps what bothered Rashi? If so, this then is the reason he made use of the midrash.

Understanding Rashi

Rashi cites the midrash to justify the use of the unusually worded phrase.

It is always wise to check the source when Rashi cites a biblical text. Look at the passage in I Kings 17. The passage tells us that Elijah reports G-d's vow that dew and rain will be withheld until further word from G-d. Elijah then went and hid in Wadi Kerit, was fed miraculously by the ravens and drank water from the wadi. Then we read (I Kings 17:7): "And it came to pass, after a while, that the brook dried up, for there was no rain in the land." The Hebrew is ויבש הנחל. Here we see a similar linguistic anamoly of water ("the brook") drying up!

The midrash is sensitive to the association between our passage and the one in Kings. Rashi quotes the midrash because in the story of Elijah the waters did dry up! The rain and dew stopped. Noah's raven "went to and fro until the waters dried up . . .". Which waters? The waters of Elijah!

The raven was actually of no service to Noah, since all it did was fly around until the waters dried. By that time Noah had already made use of the dove. So we see that the raven was really readied for another service...that for Elijah. We can now appreciate why Rashi brought the midrash in addition to the *p'shat*. But after all is said and done, this is not really *p'shat*, for the simple meaning is clear to all: "the waters dried up off the face of the earth." And that is why Rashi makes it clear that the sentence must first be understood in its simple meaning — פשוטו כמשמעו.

(See *Yerios Shlomo*)

The following Rashi is particularly instructive, for it alerts us to the importance of noting where, when and why Rashi makes a particular comment. Note that the word Rashi explains also appears in the sentence before this one (8:7), and yet there he makes no comment.

Genesis 8:8

וישלח את היונה מאתו לראות הקלו המים מעל פני האדמה.

וישלח: אין זה לשון שליחות אלא לשון שילוח, שלחה ללכת לדרכה ובזו יראה אם קלו המים שאם תמצא מנוח לא תשוב אליו.

And he sent: *Rashi:* This does not mean "sending on an errand," but "sending away," "letting go," he freed her to go where she liked, and thus he could see whether the waters abated, because if she could find a resting place she would not return to him.

What questions can you ask on this comment?

YOUR QUESTION:

QUESTIONING RASHI

We noted above that Rashi gives us the meaning of the word וישלח here, while the very same word appears in the previous sentence and there he says nothing. Why does Rashi wait until this sentence to make his comment? The more you try to answer this question and remain puzzled by it, the more you will appreciate the subtlety of Rashi's comment.

YOUR ANSWER:

What is Bothering Rashi?

An Answer: Rashi notes a linguistic problem in this sentence. The word וישלח means "setting free," like Moses' famous plea שלח את עמי "Let my people go" (Exodus 5:1). But since it means "letting go" or "setting free," then the word doesn't fit with "to see if the waters were abated." If the Torah is telling us that Noah freed the dove (as opposed to sending him on an errand), then there can be no purpose "to see if . . ." This is the difficulty Rashi alludes to.

How does his comment answer the difficulty?

Understanding Rashi

An Answer: Rashi then shows how the word "set free" can be related to "to see if . . ." This would be considered, according to our terminology, a Type I comment.

But, in a sense, this is also a Type II comment. The comment also guards us against a misunderstanding. And Rashi himself tells us this when he says: Don't translate the word וישלח thus, rather, thus. His purpose, then, is clear: to help us avoid a misunderstanding.

To understand how Rashi does this we should compare sentence 7 with sentence 8. Why is his explanation necessary on 8:8 and not on 8:7?

Your Answer:

An Answer: To answer this question you must look closely at sentence 8 and make sense out of it. "And he sent forth the dove from him to see if the waters were abated from off the face of the ground." Do you think you understand it? If you understood it, then you can certainly answer the following question! What do these words mean: "to see if the waters were abated"? Who was supposed to "see," the dove or Noah?

Your Answer:

Understanding Rashi — A Puzzle

An Answer: It would seem to be Noah, for he is the subject of the sentence, as it says, "He sent forth . . ."

But how could it mean Noah? He didn't see if the waters had abated; it was precisely because he couldn't see that he sent the dove.

So, it would seem to mean the dove was to see if the waters had abated.

But does that make any sense?

Think . . .

Answer: It certainly doesn't make sense, because the dove couldn't posssibly realize that she was being sent on a mission to see if the waters were dried up or not. The dove couldn't understand Noah's purpose in sending her out.

So it can't be Noah, for he couldn't see if the waters were dried up. And it can't be the dove because she couldn't know why she was sent. A puzzle.

DO YOU HAVE AN ANSWER?

RASHI'S EXPLANATION

This is what Rashi comes to clarify. He tells us that the dove was not "sent on an errand to see," for she couldn't possibly understand the purpose of such an errand. Rather, Noah "set the dove free" (not on a purposeful mission) so that he, Noah, could "see" (i.e., understand) whether the waters were dried up or not. How would he "see" this? "Because if she could find a resting place she would not return to him." Noah's "seeing," then, was his understanding based on an inference from the dove's behavior.

Here Rashi makes us aware of a most subtle point, one we certainly would have missed without his comment.

Now, why didn't Rashi make his comment on the previous sentence where the word וישלח first appears?

Think . . .

By this time you certainly know the answer!

YOUR ANSWER:

Answer: Rashi did not make his comment on 8:7 because all it says is "Noah sent out the raven" and no purpose is mentioned, as in 8:8. Without this, there is no source of confusion and, thus, no need to comment and clarify.

This is a beautiful illustration of Rashi's exquisite sensitivity to the finer points of the text.

(See Gur Aryeh)

Searching for meaning in this comment alerts us to the subtle differences between apparently similar verses.

Genesis 9:17

ויאמר אלוקים אל נח זאת אות הברית אשר הקמתי ביני ובין כל בשר אשר על הארץ.

זאת אות הברית: הראהו הקשת ואמר לו: הרי האות שאמרתי.

This is the sign of the covenant: *Rashi:* He showed him the rainbow and said to him: "This is the sign of which I have spoken."

QUESTIONING RASHI

What question comes to mind as you read this Rashi comment?

YOUR QUESTION:

A Question: What is Rashi telling us? What does he add to our understanding that we hadn't already known? Rashi's comment appears to say the same thing as the sentence in the Torah. What does he mean when he says, "This is the sign of which I have spoken"? Something is bothering Rashi. What is it?

YOUR ANSWER:

WHAT IS BOTHERING RASHI?

Hint:

See sentence 9:12.

Does this help you understand what is bothering Rashi?

YOUR ANSWER:

An Answer: This sentence appears redundant, for G-d already said to Noah (9:12): "This is the sign . . ."

How does Rashi's comment deal with the redundancy?

YOUR ANSWER:

Understanding Rashi

An Answer: When we compare sentence 12 with this sentence, we see that the words "This is the sign" have a slightly different meaning in each case. In sentence 12, they are intended to tell Noah what the sign is: "My bow have I set in the cloud." But in our sentence the words "this is the sign" can only mean that G-d actually showed him the rainbow in the sky. When Rashi says, "this is the sign of which I have spoken," he is acknowledging the earlier sentence and in this way shows that sentence 9:17 is not redundant; rather it gives Noah additional clarity by showing him the rainbow itself. Rashi's point, then, is that the identical words are not mere repetition.

(See Be'er Yitzchak; Havanas HaMikra)

פרשת לך לך

The following Rashi comment is rather straightforward, yet it has several nuances that are noteworthy.

Genesis 12:1

ויאמר ה' אל אברם לך לך מארצך וממולדתך ומבית אביך אל הארץ אשר אראך.

> **לך לך:** להנאתך ולטובתך, שם אעשך לגוי גדול, כאן אי אתה זוכה לבנים. ועוד, שאודיע טבעך בעולם.
>
> **You go:** *Rashi:* For your own benefit, for your own good. There I will make you a great nation whereas here you will not merit the privilege of having children. And furthermore I shall make known your character throughout the world.

QUESTIONING RASHI

What bothers you about this Rashi? If you could ask Rashi about it, what would you ask him?

YOUR QUESTION:

Questions: The meaning of the verse seems obvious: Go leave your country. Why does Rashi elaborate so much? What in these words is bothering Rashi?

Hint:

Look at the *dibbur hamaschil.*

YOUR ANSWER:

WHAT IS BOTHERING RASHI?

An Answer: The words לך לך, "You go" mean literally "Go for yourself," which implies, as Rashi points out, "going for your own benefit." But this is inappropriate here, since Abram is being asked to do a difficult deed — to leave his homeland and family — which appears to be to his detriment, not to his benefit.

UNDERSTANDING RASHI

Rashi therefore explains that Abram's leaving his country will, indeed, turn out to be to his benefit.

A DEEPER LOOK

This doesn't exhaust our examination of Rashi's comment. If Rashi only wanted to tell us that Abram's leaving would benefit him because he would become a great nation, it would have sufficed to end with those words. Why does Rashi continue with "Here you will not merit having children"?

WHAT IS STILL BOTHERING RASHI?

Clue:

Note that part of Rashi's comment is a direct quote from the verse. The words אעשך לגוי גדול come from the Torah text. Rashi, however, adds the word שם, "there." This should be a clue to you. Remember our Type II comment? (See chapter *Appreciating Rashi*.) This is a fine example of such a comment; by adding just one word Rashi intends to warn us of a likely misunderstanding.

From which misunderstanding is he guarding us?

Think! Read the first two sentences and clearly explain their meaning to yourself.

YOUR ANSWER:

UNDERSTANDING THE MISUNDERSTANDING

An Answer: The two sentences parallel cause and effect: Abram is told to leave his land (cause) and the effect will be that he will become a great nation. "Becoming a great nation" is the result of "going forth from your land." But this can be misleading. The Torah seems to be saying that G-d is promising to make of Abram a great people as a reward for his leaving his father's house.

But Rashi thinks this is an incorrect understanding of the Torah's intent and it is regarding this error that he wants to alert us. He inserts the word שם to tell us that Abram's becoming a great people is a consequence of his leaving his father's house but not a reward. That is the force of the word שם in this comment: "There" I will make you a great nation and not "here" in *chutz l'aretz*. It is the Land of Israel that gives Abram the merit to have children, not his fulfilling the command of leaving his homeland. Here — in his father's house — he will not have that merit.

Support for Rashi's Interpretation

But how does Rashi know this? Maybe, in fact, it is meant as a reward.

Your Answer:

An Answer: The answer must come from common sense. Such an extraordinary promise (of becoming a great nation, etc.) is not likely to be the reward for a mundane act like leaving one's country. Remember Abram was already seventy-five years old. We would expect him to be able to leave his father's house without much difficulty. Seventy-five years of age is hardly time to experience separation anxiety! Thus Rashi concludes that G-d's making Abram into a great people was a consequence (and not a reward) of his leaving; something that could happen only in the Land of Israel. As he says, "Here you will not merit the privilege of having children."

(See *Sefer Zikaron*)

This Rashi comment gives us some insight about how Rashi sees p'shat and drash.

Genesis 12:5

ויקח אברם את שרי אשתו ואת לוט בן אחיו ואת כל רכושם אשר רכשו ואת הנפש אשר עשו בחרן ויצאו ללכת ארצה כנען ויבאו ארצה כנען.

אשר עשו בחרן: שהכניסן תחת כנפי השכינה, אברהם מגייר את האנשים ושרה מגיירת הנשים ומעלה עליהם הכתוב כאלו עשאו ופשוטו של מקרא: עבדים ושפחות שקנו להם כמו ״עשה את כל הכבוד הזה״ (שם ל״א) ״וישראל עושה חיל״ (במד׳ כ״ד) לשון קונה וכונס.

[The souls] which they had gotten (lit., "had made") in Haran: Rashi: Which they had brought beneath the wings of the Shechinah. Abraham converted the men and Sarah converted the women and Scripture accounts it unto them as if they had made them. However the plain sense of the text is that it refers to menservants and to the maid-servants whom they had acquired for themselves. The word עשו is used here as in Gen. 31:1: "he has acquired (עשה) all this wealth," and Num. 24:8: "And Israel acquires (עושה) wealth" — an expression for acquiring and amassing.

What questions would you ask here?

YOUR QUESTION:

QUESTIONING RASHI

This comment is made up of midrash and *p'shat*.

Therefore we might ask:

1. What in the text is bothering Rashi that prompts his comment?

2. Why the need for the midrash — isn't *p'shat* enough?

3. And why the midrash before the *p'shat*?

YOUR ANSWER TO THE FIRST QUESTION:

What Is Bothering Rashi?

An Answer: This should not have been too difficult to figure out. From Rashi's answer we can confidently assume that he was bothered by the use of the word עשו "they made." Its use in this sentence is unusual. You do not "make" souls! His *p'shat* interpretation, that the word means "acquire," would seem most reasonable, yet he is bothered by several things, which prompts him to offer another interpretation. Can you figure out what about the *p'shat* interpretation might make it somewhat inadequate?

Your Answer:

An Answer: If the servants were acquired as chattel like their other purchases, then why does the Torah not include them under the same phrase used for possessions ("all their substance")? And if we think that servants should be listed separately from inanimate objects, why wasn't the same term used, i.e., "purchased" (רכשו) for them, instead of the unusual word "made" (עשו)?

See how the midrash answers these difficulties. The servants were not made or even acquired in the normal sense; rather they were converted (spiritually "made") to monotheism. Certainly a very different situation from that of Abram's nonhuman possessions.

But, since this midrash answers so perfectly the textual problems, is it not really *p'shat*? Why does Rashi bring another interpretation which he labels *p'shat*?

Think . . .

Your Answer:

Rashi's P'shuto Shel Mikrah

An Answer: What differentiates *p'shat* from *drash*? This is not easy; the lines between the two are by no means clear and unequivocal. We would suggest that one difference is that *p'shat* deals with the written text, while midrash is not bound exclusively to what the text says. So if Abraham had, in fact, converted so many people, we would expect to find these converted souls referred to somewhere in the Torah. But they are not mentioned anywhere in the Torah. That is why this is considered *drash*.

Why does Rashi bring the midrash first, before the *p'shat*?

Your Answer:

An Answer: I would suggest that this midrash — because of the unusual use of the word "made," because of the separate reference to souls and because of our knowledge of Abraham as a pioneer in spreading the monotheistic idea - all these make this midrash very close to *p'shat*, and thus Rashi brings it first.

[Note: Rashi speaks of conversions by both Abraham and Sarah because the word עשו is in the plural]

(See *Maskil L'Dovid*)

A beautiful Rashi comment that subtly and skillfully reframes the Torah's words, enabling us to understand them better.

Genesis 15:1

אחר הדברים האלה היה דבר ה' אל אברם במחזה לאמר אל
תירא אברם אנכי מגן לך שכרך הרבה מאד.

אחר הדברים האלה: כל מקום שנאמר "אחר" סמוך, "אחרי"
— מופלג.

אחר הדברים האלה. אחר שנעשה לו נס זה, שהרג את המלכים
והיה דואג ואומר שמא קבלתי שכר על כל צדקותי לכך אמר לו
המקום אל תירא אברם אנכי מגן לך מן העונש שלא תענש על
כל אותן נפשות שהרגת. ומה שאתה דואג על קבול שכרך, שכרך
הרבה מאוד.

After (אחר) these things: *Rashi:* Wherever the term אחר is used, it means immediately after the preceding event, while אחרי means a long time afterwards.

After these things: *Rashi:* After this miracle has been wrought for him in that he killed the kings and he was worried, saying, "Perhaps I have already received reward for all my good deeds," then G-d said to him, "FEAR NOT ABRAM. I AM YOUR SHIELD" against punishment; for you will not be punished on account of all these people whom you have killed. And as for your being worried regarding the receipt of reward, "YOUR REWARD WILL BE EXCEEDINGLY GREAT."

QUESTIONING RASHI

This is a long comment. Rashi fills in the text with additional information; he tells us that Abram was worried and what he was worried about.

What questions can you ask on this comment?

YOUR QUESTIONS:

A Question: What purpose do these additions serve?

Do you have an answer?

YOUR ANSWER:

WHAT IS BOTHERING RASHI?

Rashi has already told us that this divine vision came immediately after the preceding event, which was Abram's military victory over the four kings. The words "After these things ...[G-d said] Fear not .. your reward is very great" clearly implies that there is some relationship between the two events — the victory on the one hand and the vision on the other. Rashi is puzzled by the connection between these two events.

What else do you find strange about this sentence? See the verse in context.

YOUR ANSWER:

An Answer: After Abram soundly defeated the four kings, G-d tells him "Fear not"!

This certainly is strange. G-d didn't see the need to embolden Abram before his battle, so why should He now, after Abram was victorious? How does Rashi's comment deal with this?

YOUR ANSWER:

UNDERSTANDING RASHI

Rashi tells us that Abram saw this victory not as a personal accomplishment, but rather as a gift from G-d and because of this he began to worry. He worried that perhaps G-d's military assistance was his reward for his righteousness and that now he stood emptied of his merits. This caused him worry and thus G-d said "Fear not." This explains both why G-d said "Fear not" and what the connection is with the first part of the sentence, "After these things."

A CLOSER LOOK AT RASHI

If we analyze Rashi we see that he says three things:

1. Abram worried about losing his merits

2. G-d said he would not be punished for killing people in battle.

3. Abram worried that he would have no further rewards.

See that G-d said three things to Abram:

1. Fear not

2. I will shield you

3. You reward is very great.

Notice that the three fears that Rashi enumerates parallel the three statements in the Torah.

G-d's words		*Rashi's comment*
Fear not	❖	Worry about losing merits
I will shield you	❖	Worry about being punished
Your reward is great	❖	Worry about having no future reward

A DEEPER LOOK

Rashi has made a subtle change in the understanding of this verse. Can you see what it is?

YOUR ANSWER:

An Answer: Rashi reframes our whole understanding of this sentence by a subtle change in translation. He changes יראה, "fear," to דאגה, "worry" . While "fear" has a physical sense (attack from without), "worry" has a psychological connotation (being punished, not being rewarded, etc.) We now perceive the meaning of this sentence differently. "Fear not" means "worry not." We understand that Abram was not fearful of suffering physical harm; he was rather worried about more spiritual concerns. Now it makes sense that G-d's assurances come after Abram's waging war and not before, because his concerns were the by-product of his victory.

(See Be'er Yitzchak)

This comment is a fine example of Rashi's sensitivity to both words and concept. The meaning of the statement of Abraham's belief in G-d's promise may seem obvious, but Rashi sees a more profound point to comment on.

Genesis 15:6

והאמן בהי ויחשבה לו צדקה.

והאמן בהי: לא שאל לו אות על זאת, אבל על ירושת הארץ שאל לו אות ואמר במה אדע.

And he believed in G-d: *Rashi:* He did not ask Him for a sign regarding this, but in respect to the promise that he would possess the Land (15:7) he did ask for a sign, saying, "By what sign shall I know [that I will possess it]?"

QUESTIONING RASHI

What question would you ask on this Rashi?

YOUR QUESTION:

Question: Rashi's comment points out the difference between Abraham's re-actions to being told he will have children and being told he will inherit the Land of Israel. But this is all in the text itself, and thus quite obvious. The Torah makes it quite clear that in one case (the promise of children) Abraham accepts (believes) G-d's promise without asking for evidence, while in the second (the promise of the land) he asks for evidence.

Why does Rashi find it necessary to point this out?

WHAT IS BOTHERING RASHI?

An Answer: The Torah says that Abraham believed G-d. How utterly superflu-ous! Why should he not believe G-d's word? G-d was speaking to him, directly. If Abraham believed that the prophecy he was personally experiencing was authentic, would he possibly think that G-d was putting him on? Rashi implicitly asks: What could the Torah mean when it says "He believed in G-d."

How does Rashi's comment deal with this?

YOUR ANSWER:

UNDERSTANDING RASHI

Since Rashi realized that a statement certifying Abraham's faith in G-d's promise is gratuitous, he interpreted the statement about faith in a slightly different way. It was not a matter of faith, Rashi tells us, it was rather one of having or not having some sign of G-d's intention. Regarding the promise of children, Abraham did not need a symbolic act which he could hold onto. Not so regarding the promise of the Land. Here Abraham, while having perfect faith, nevertheless asked for some sign. He received the Covenant Between the Pieces. Rashi's comment thus has the effect of reinterpreting Abraham's reactions to the two promises from the unreasonable faith/scepticism dichotomy to the more understandable sign/no sign dichotomy, thereby avoiding (or voiding) completely the issue of Abraham's faith.

(See Devek Tov)

פרשת וירא

Following is a typical comment that makes use of a midrash based on problems in the text.

Genesis 18:1

וירא אליו ה׳ באלני ממרא והוא ישב פתח האהל כחם היום.

> **וירא אליו:** לבקר את החולה, אמר רבי חמא בר חנינא, יום שלישי למילתו היה ובא הקב״ה ושאל בשלומו.
>
> **And [the L-rd] appeared to him:** *Rashi:* To visit the sick. Rebbe Hama, son of Chanina, said: it was the third day after his circumcision and the Holy One, Blessed Be He, came and inquired after his health.

In analyzing this comment, what question would you ask?

YOUR QUESTION:

QUESTIONING RASHI

A question which is always appropriate when Rashi cites a midrash is: What prompted Rashi to bring this midrash of Rebbe Hama? Why the need for it? Notice that although there is an important moral lesson to be learned here, i.e., the importance of visiting the sick, nevertheless Rashi would not bring this in his commentary unless something about the text made it necessary.

Another question we would ask is: How does Rashi conclude that G-d was visiting the sick? Where in the text is this even hinted at?

Rashi bases his comment on two anomalies in the text. Can you find them?

What is bothering him?

YOUR ANSWER:

WHAT IS BOTHERING RASHI?

An Answer: The first point is to be found in Rashi's *dibbur hamaschil.*

"And [the L-rd] appeared to him." To whom? we would ask. You don't begin a new section with a pronoun! The use of the pronoun directs our attention back to the previous section, the last time Abraham is mentioned by name. It is there that the Torah speaks of Abraham's circumcision. And we can imagine that circumcision for a ninety-nine-year-old man would be a painful experience and require a period of recuperation. This, in fact, is what Rebbe Hama said.

The second point comes from an examination of this sentence. We are told that G-d appeared to Abraham, but nothing follows. There is no recorded message in this Divine appearance. This is quite unusual. Compare, for example, Genesis 12:7 or 17:1 or 26:2. In each case the appearance of G-d is followed by a Divine utterance. Not so in our case.

Putting these two points together, Rashi arrives at his interpretation.

How does his comment deal with this difficulty?

YOUR ANSWER:

UNDERSTANDING RASHI

On the basis of the connection with the last chapter, which tells of Abraham's circumcision, and the absence of any Divine utterance in this vision, Rashi concludes that the Divine appearance must be for the sake of visiting Abraham in his sick state; such a visit requires no utterance, the Divine presence being sufficient.

A CLOSER LOOK AT REBBE HAMA'S DRASH

Rebbe Hama assumes it was the third day after the circumcision based on the story of the people of Shechem who circumcised themselves. See Genesis 34:25: "And it was on the third day when they were sore, etc." We see from here that after circumcision, the third day is the most painful.

(See Mishmeres HaKodesh)

The following Rashi comment is deceptively simple, its point easily missed. In fact it is a piece of exegetic artistry: succinct, subtle and enlightening.

Genesis 18:9

ויאמרו אליו איה שרה אשתך ויאמר הנה באהל.

הנה באהל: צנועה היא.
Behold in the tent: *Rashi:* She is modest.

What would you ask of this Rashi comment?

YOUR QUESTION:

QUESTIONING RASHI

This Rashi is a bit difficult to question. Our first inclination is to say that nothing is bothering Rashi, and to accept his comment as a lesson about Sarah's modesty. The fact that she remained in the tent indicates her modesty.

But, we must remember that Rashi never just informs us, no matter how enlightening the information may be. Again we stress: Rashi doesn't comment unless the text urges him to do so. Thus we ask: What in the text urges him to make this comment?

Clue #1:

You must look at the whole sentence to understand this.

YOUR ANSWER:

If you haven't found an answer, here is another clue.

Clue #2:

You should ask yourself, what relevance does Sarah's modesty have to the question which Abraham was asked: "Where is Sarah your wife?" His answer that she was in the tent should have been sufficient. Why must Rashi add that she is modest?

What in the sentence forces Rashi to make his comment?

The sentence reads: ויאמרו אליו איה שרה אשתך ויאמר הנה באהל

And they said to him: Where is Sarah your wife? And he said: Behold, in the tent. Rashi's sensitivity to the nuances in Hebrew are at the basis of this comment.

What nuance?

YOUR ANSWER:

WHAT IS BOTHERING RASHI?

An Answer: The word איה (where is) is unusual here. It does not mean "Where is Sarah?" as it is usually translated. If that is what the angels intended to ask, they would have used the word איפה. When Joseph asks (Genesis 37:16): "Where (איפה) are [my brothers] shepherding?" he wants to know where they are and uses איפה.

The use of איה and not איפה is likely what is bothering Rashi.

How does his comment deal with this?

YOUR ANSWER:

UNDERSTANDING RASHI

Rashi understood that the word איה is used when one wants to know why someone is not where he is expected to be. As in אי הבל אחיך "where is Abel your brother?" (Genesis 4:9). G-d wasn't asking Cain where Abel was; He was asking "why isn't he here?" Likewise, in our case, the angels were asking: Why is not Sarah here with you? This nuance prompted Rashi's comment.

In that case, Abraham's answer that Sarah was in the tent wasn't a sufficient answer to the intention of their question. Saying that she is modest explains why she isn't outside with Abraham. That is an appropriate answer to their question. That is what Rashi is adding by his brief comment.

SUPPORT FOR RASHI'S INTERPRETATION

In addition to this linguistic nuance, can you find logical support for Rashi's comment?

YOUR ANSWER:

An Answer: We do not find the angels asking any further questions about Sarah. If, in fact, they were interested in knowing where she was, we could assume that they wanted to call her. But the angels make no further requests regarding Sarah, indicating that they only wanted to know why she wasn't outside. Once they knew, they continued their conversation with Abraham alone.

We now see how Rashi's comment is necessary and fitting. By answering that Sarah was in the tent because she was modest, he has answered their question, "Why isn't she here?" (איה).

An Additional Point — the *Dibbur Hamaschil*

According to this understanding of Rashi, his interpretation is based on the word איה, yet this word does not appear in the *dibbur hamaschil*. While all Rashi interpreters agree that his *dibbur hamaschil* is important to his comment, some believe that the *dibbur hamaschil* is always at the center of Rashi's focus. In the understanding we offered (based on the supercommentary *Havanas HaMikra*) the *dibbur hamaschil* is not central to the understanding. For this reason, there are other interpretations.

Another Interpretation, Based on the *Dibbur Hamaschil*

The use of the word הנה appears to be unnecessary. It adds nothing, for Abraham could just as well have said באהל, "in the tent" and his answer would have been just as adequate. Why then the use of הנה? This word implies "certainly," as if to say, "why even ask?" She is not outside for she is modest. So Rashi concludes that Abraham implied Sarah's modesty by adding the word הנה.

This understanding of Rashi focuses on the *dibbur hamaschil* as the clue to his meaning. From this example, the student can see that understanding Rashi does not necessarily lead to one unequivocal answer.

(See *Havanas HaMikra; Divrei Dovid*)

The following comment illustrates Rashi's precise choice of words, so

characteristic of his commentary.

Genesis 22:1

ויהי אחר הדברים האלה והאלקים נסה את אברהם ויאמר אליו
אברהם ויאמר הנני.

הנני: כך היא עניתם של חסידים, לשון ענוה הוא ולשון זימון.
Here I am: *Rashi:* Such is the answer of the pious, an
expression of humility and readiness.

Have you got a question on this Rashi? What is it?

YOUR QUESTION:

QUESTIONING RASHI

Answer: Why the need to explain a familiar word like הנני (previously used
in Genesis 6:17; 9:9)? Rashi does not define or explain every word,
only unusual words or common words that require special attention.

What about the text is bothering him?

YOUR ANSWER:

WHAT IS BOTHERING RASHI?

The word הנני literally means הנה אני "Behold, I am." It is a confirmation
or emphasis of one's presence (see, for example, Samuel I 3:4–5) or
one's intention (see Genesis 6:17 and 9:9). But if G-d is speaking to
Abraham, He is obviously aware of his presence. Rashi is bothered by
the word's inappropriateness here. How does his comment answer this
question?

YOUR ANSWER:

UNDERSTANDING RASHI

An Answer: Rashi's comment explains that the term has a specific meaning,
i.e., not that Abraham is present — which is obvious — but that he
is emotionally present, i.e., ready to do G-d's bidding.

A Closer Look at Rashi

We can appreciate a finer point of Rashi's commentary by comparing this comment with the Rashi on Genesis 37:13. There Israel says to Joseph his son, "Are not your brothers shepherding in Shechem? Go and I will send you to them. And he said: Here I am (הנני)."

Rashi comments there: (Genesis 37:13)

> **הנני:** לשון ענוה וזריזות נזדרז למצות אביו ואף על פי שהיה
> יודע באחיו ששונאין אותו.
>
> **Here I am:** *Rashi:* An expression of humility and alacrity. He was zealous to perform his father's bidding, even though he was aware that his brothers hated him.

Here, too, Rashi comments because the word הנני cannot have its usual meaning, a confirmation of presence: Since Israel is talking directly to Joseph, he certainly knows that he is present.

It is instructive to compare the wording of these two comments. Notice the similarities and differences.

What are they?

Your Answer:

Comparing Rashi Comments

An Answer: In both comments Rashi uses the term ענוה, "humility," but in the previous comment, he adds the word זימון, "readiness," while in the case of Joseph, he uses the word זריזות, "alacrity."

Why? Explain the difference between the two situations.

Think . . .

Understanding Rashi

The choice of words is precise, for Abraham answered הנני *before* he knew what G-d would require of him. His הנני meant he was ready (זימון) for whatever G-d would ask of him. Joseph, on the other hand, knew full well the danger of the mission he was being sent on before he answered הנני, since he was asked to go to his brothers who hated him. His use of the word הנני meant that he would not hesitate, he would respond with alacrity to do his father's wish, even though it was dangerous. Here the word הנני must mean "with alacrity."

The slight difference in choice of words illustrates Rashi's verbal precision — one of the hallmarks of his commentary.

(See Be'er Yitzchak)

Following are two more Rashi comments which explain the same word in different ways.

Genesis 23:11

לא אדני שמעני השדה נתתי לך ומערה אשר בו לך נתתיה לעיני
בני עמי נתתיה לך קבר מתך.

נתתי לך: הרי היא כמו שנתתיה לך.
I have given it to you: *Rashi:* Behold, it is as if I have already given it to you.

What question would you ask on this comment?

YOUR QUESTION:

QUESTIONING RASHI

Question: The meaning of the words Rashi explains — נתתי לך — are quite simple; why the need to comment on them? What's bothering Rashi?

YOUR ANSWER:

WHAT IS BOTHERING RASHI?

An Answer: The word נתתי is in the past tense. And even though Ephron makes the point — and repeats it — that the field is already given to Abraham, in fact no transfer has been made. The field is still in Ephron's possession. It would be more correct to say "I will give you" or "I give you." Why the use of the past tense? This is what is bothering Rashi.

How does he answer this?

UNDERSTANDING RASHI

Rashi explains that the past tense here, נתתי, does not literally describe an action in the past; rather it is meant to emphasize Ephron's resoluteness in this matter. He tells Abraham that he has made the decision to give him the field and, therefore, it is already as good as done.

Now compare this with Rashi's comment on the same word which appears again two sentences further:

Genesis 23:13

וידבר אל עפרון באזני עם הארץ לאמר אך אם אתה לו שמעני
נתתי כסף השדה קח ממני ואקברה את מתי שמה.

נתתי: מוכן הוא אצלי והלואי נתתי לך כבר.
I have given: *Rashi:* I have the money ready and I only wish that I had already given it to you.

In light of our question and answer on the previous Rashi (23:11), questioning this comment should be easy.

What would you ask?

YOUR QUESTION:

QUESTIONING RASHI

Question: Here, too, the word נתתי is in the past tense. Although Abraham says, "I have given the money . . .," he had not really given any money. In fact, his very next words, "Take it from me," indicate clearly that the money had yet to be given. So, again, Rashi is reacting to the inappropriate use of the word נתתי.

COMPARING RASHI COMMENTS

Once you see these two interpretations, the next question should be obvious:

What is it?

YOUR QUESTION:

An obvious question is: Why does Rashi give different interpretations for the same word?

YOUR ANSWER:

Understanding Rashi

Several answers have been suggested here.

Answer #1: Ephron (24:11) is talking about giving his land to Abraham, while Abraham (24:13) is talking about giving his money to Ephron. Land is not given from hand to hand; all that is necessary is the owner's consent. Ephron says, You have my consent, therefore "It is as if it is already given." On the other hand, Abraham is talking about giving money, and money must be actually handed over before the deal is closed. Thus Abraham can only say, "The money is ready; I only wish that I had already given it to you."

There is another difference between the situations of Ephron and Abraham which would explain why Rashi offers different comments for the same word. Can you think what it might be?

YOUR ANSWER:

Answer #2: Ephron is the owner and controls the transaction, while Abraham is the buyer and can only hope the seller will consent to sell. When Abraham says "I wish I had already given it," we would say: Well then, give it! But of course Abraham can not, unless and until Ephron first consents. Thus, all Abraham can say is: "I wish I had already given it," meaning, I wish you would consent. This alone can explain the different interpretations Rashi offers for the same word.

Note how grammar, compositional style and contextual meaning are all very important to Rashi. He notices irregularities and inconsistencies, and comments on them.

(See *Devek Tov; Mesiach Ilmim*)

In the following comment, Rashi uses Gematria (a non-p'shat interpretation — the numerical value). We see how this too must answer to the basic criteria of relevance and contextual fit. Rashi frequently uses Midrash and Gematria in his commentary, but he does so only if the text itself is a source of puzzlement. Finding the puzzling element is not always easy.

Genesis 24:1

ואברהם זקן בא בימים והי׳ ברך את אברהם בכל.

ברך את אברהם בכל: בכל עולה בגימטריא בן, ומאחר שהיה
לו בן, היה צריך להשיאו אשה.

He blessed Abraham with everything: *Rashi:* The gematria of the word בכל, with everything, (52) is equal to that of בן, a son, (52) — [suggesting that G-d has blessed Abraham with a son] and since he had a son, he had to find him a wife.

QUESTIONING RASHI

Considering that Rashi is basically interested in *p'shat*, what can you ask about this comment?

YOUR QUESTION:

Question: What prompts Rashi to abandon *p'shat* and resort to *gematria*?

Is there any problem with the sentence? Any problem with the context within which the sentence occurs?

YOUR ANSWER:

WHAT IS BOTHERING RASHI?

Answer: Rashi is puzzled by the relatedness of this opening sentence (of chapter 24) to the rest of the chapter that follows, (one of the longest chapters in the whole Torah). What has the fact that Abraham was blessed with everything have to do with sending his servant on a mission to find a wife for his son Isaac?

Do you have an answer?

YOUR ANSWER:

UNDERSTANDING RASHI

Rashi finds the connection between the opening words "And G-d blessed Abraham with everything (בכל)" and the rest of the chapter in the *gematria* of the word בכל, which is the same as בן, son. "G-d blessed Abraham with a son" . . . and therefore he must now find him a wife.

SUPPORT FOR RASHI'S INTERPERTATION

Support for abandoning *p'shat* (that "G-d blessed Abraham with everything") can be found by comparison to another sentence in this chapter which is similar in meaning to our sentence here.

Which sentence, and how does it support Rashi? Search the chapter.

YOUR ANSWER:

An Answer: Look at sentence 24:35 where the servant tells Rebecca's family about his mission. There he says, "And G-d blessed my lord greatly (מאוד . . .)." Compare this to our sentence "And G-d blessed Abraham with everything (בכל)." Between the two, the servant's phrase is more accurate. Our phrase is certainly an exaggeration — after all Abraham didn't really have EVERYTHING. Thus, Rashi realized that בכל was an odd word in this context. This, together with the fact that the simple sense of the phrase has no connection with the chapter as a whole, leads Rashi to make use of the *gematria* to explain our text.

A DEEPER LOOK AT RASHI

Now if, in fact, the word בן, "son," is to be more appropriate than the word בכל, "everything," the next question should be obvious.

What is it?

YOUR QUESTION:

QUESTIONING THE DRASH

Why didn't the Torah use the word בן? Why did it use the apparently less appropriate word בכל?

Your Answer:

Understanding the Drash

The Torah uses the word בכל because this reflects the deeper significance of having a son in Abraham's eyes. For him a son was EVERYTHING! See how Abraham speaks to G-d above (Genesis 15:3): "And Abram said, Behold to me Thou hast given no seed: and behold the one born in my house [the servant] will inherit me." We see that without a son Abraham has nothing, since all he acquired in his lifetime, both materially and spiritually, will pass over to his servant. Nothing will be left to the house of Abraham — neither seed nor possessions.

Lesson: Even midrashim and gematrios are in some way anchored in the text; if Rashi uses them they probably answer some difficulty in the text.

(See Gur Aryeh)

This comment picks up on apparent redundancies in the Torah's wording.

Genesis 24:10

ויקח העבד עשרה גמלים מגמלי אדניו וילך וכל טוב אדניו בידו
ויקם וילך אל ארם נהרים אל עיר נחור.

מגמלי אדניו: נכרין היו משאר גמלים, שהיו יוצאין זמומין מפני הגזל שלא ירעו בשדות אחרים.
Of his master's camels: *Rashi:* These were distinguished from other camels by going out muzzled to avoid robbery — that they should not graze in other people's fields.

Questioning Rashi

The basic question must be asked here. What is it?

Your Question:

What Is Bothering Rashi?

Extra, unnecessary words in the Torah text usually draw Rashi's attention. The *dibbur hamaschil* — מגמלי אדוניו — are superfluous; whose camels would Abraham's servant take if not those of his master? Rashi is bothered by the superfluous words.

How does his comment explain them?

YOUR ANSWER:

UNDERSTANDING RASHI

Rashi's comment tells us that these words are not redundant; they tell us that Abraham's camels looked different (because of their muzzles) and thus the servant took camels that everyone recognized as "his master's camels." The words are necessary for they convey an important moral message.

A CLOSER LOOK

How did Rashi know that the muzzles were the distinguishing characteristic of Abraham's camels? Although we certainly would not suspect Abraham of robbery, we should find some support for the assertion that Abraham's camels were muzzled. What in the text supports this assumption? Read on further in the story to find the evidence.

YOUR ANSWER:

SUPPORT FOR RASHI'S INTEPRETATION

See Genesis 24:32

ויבא האיש הביתה ויפתח הגמלים ויתן תבן וגו'.

And the man came into the house and he unmuzzled the camels and gave straw, etc.

We see that they were in fact, muzzled. Why would he muzzle them on a long trip? Rashi tells us: Abraham's fear that they might graze in fields along the way.

Rashi's comment both supports the text he interprets and, in turn, finds support in the text.

(See Mizrachi)

Again subtleties in the text draw Rashi's attention.

Genesis 24:17

וירץ העבד לקראתה ויאמר הגמיאיני נא מעט מים מכדך.

וירץ העבד לקראתה: לפי שראה שעלו המים לקראתה.
And the servant ran towards her: *Rashi:* Because he saw that the waters rose up towards her.

This is certainly a strange comment. What would you ask about it?

YOUR QUESTION:

QUESTIONING RASHI

Why does Rashi bring the midrash?

What is bothering him here?

What difficulty in the text prompted him to make use of a midrash?

YOUR ANSWER:

WHAT IS BOTHERING RASHI?

Rashi's *dibbur hamaschil* is our clue. And the servant ran — וירץ העבד.

Why did he run? That is the question; he could just as easily have strolled over to the girl. Rashi's comment is meant to explain this strange behavior. Rashi's comment tells us that he ran towards her because he saw something very unusual about this girl — the waters rose towards her!

Now, what could you ask about the midrash itself?

YOUR QUESTION:

QUESTIONING THE MIDRASH

It's against the law of gravity for the water to rise up, even for Rebecca. We would expect her to bend down to draw up the water.

Question: On what basis does the midrash (and Rashi) conclude that this miraculous event actually happened?

Can you find support for the midrash in the story?

Look over the section.

YOUR ANSWER:

SUPPORT FOR THE MIDRASH _____

The midrash noticed that it says here: "And she went down to the well and filled her pitcher" — ותרד העינה ותמלא כדה. Previously it said: "And the daughters of the city come out to *draw* water" — ובנות אנשי העיר יצאות לשאב מים (24:13). And in 24:20, "And she ran again unto the well to *draw* water . . ." — ותרץ עוד אל הבאר לשאב . . .

In each case it says they "drew water."

In our sentence, on the other hand, it omits the drawing of water and says only that she filled her pitcher. Why? Because the waters rose up to her; she had no need to draw the waters.

This analysis fulfills the basic requirements of an in-depth understanding of Rashi:

1) What difficulty in the text prompted Rashi to make his comment — the comment being, in effect, his answer to that question?

2) What in the text supports the particular answer he offers?

(See Ramban)

For a change, we will look at a straightforward Rashi comment. His purpose here is clear: to define an unusual word.

Genesis: 24:63

ויצא יצחק לשוח בשדה לפנות ערב וישא עיניו וירא והנה גמלים באים.

לשוח: לשון תפילה כמו ישפוך שיחו (תהלים ק"ב.א).

To meditate: *Rashi:* This means to pray, as we find, "when he poured forth his prayer (שיח)" (Psalms 102:1).

One of Rashi's tasks in his commentary is to define or clarify the meaning of unfamiliar words. Here he tells us the meaning of the word שיח. Lest the student think that the meaning of this word, though rare, is nevertheless obvious, I would warn against such rash assumptions!

The word has caused controversy among the commentators. Ibn Ezra, for example, says שיח means "bush" — Isaac was walking among the bushes when he saw the camels coming. The Rashbam, Rashi's grandson (who was familiar with Rashi's commentary and probably one of the first to learn Chumash-with-Rashi *with* Rashi!), disagrees with his grandfather. He says that Isaac was planting trees! He bases his *p'shat* on Genesis 2:5 where it says, "And every plant of the field . . ." . . . וכל שיח השדה.

We can now appreciate that Rashi was translating this word as "to pray" in order to exclude the other possible interpretations. Realizing that Rashi gives one intrepretation of the word לשיח while Ibn Ezra and the Rashbam give other interpretations,

What question would you ask of Rashi?

YOUR QUESTION:

QUESTIONING RASHI

Question: We would want to know why Rashi chose this interpretation over the others, particularly since the word שיח has already been used in the Torah (Genesis 2:5) to mean "plants."

Can you find support for Rashi's interpretation?

Clue:

Look at the complete sentence.

YOUR ANSWER:

UNDERSTANDING RASHI

An Answer: It says: "And Isaac went out to meditate in the field at the turn of evening . . ." If he was planting trees or strolling among the bushes, what difference does it make what time of day it was? If, on the other hand, he was praying, then the time is significant. Jews pray three times a day, based on the quote, "Evening, morning and noon I will pray (אשיחה)" (Psalms 55:18). Here we see that the word שיחה is brought in connection with evening time, ערב. Thus Rashi chose prayer over planting because of the contextual clues in the sentence.

Note: Rashi quotes the last part of the sentence in Psalms 102:1. It is wise always to check the quote at its source, to see the full sentence. There it says, "A prayer (תפילה) of the afflicted when he faints and pours out his שיח before the L-rd." Here it is evident that שיח means prayer.

(See Karnei Ohr on Ibn Ezra)

See how a logical analysis of the text leads us inevitably to Rashi's comment.

Genesis 25:22

ויתרצצו הבנים בקרבה ותאמר אם כן למה זה אנכי ותלך לדרש
את ה'.

> **ותלך לדרוש:** לבית מדרשו של שם.
> **And she went to inquire:** *Rashi:* To the Beis Medrash of Shem.

By this time you should find it easy to question this Rashi.

YOUR QUESTION:

QUESTIONING RASHI

Question: Why does Rashi reject the simplest interpretation — that she spoke to G-d directly (in prayer)? Why the need to say she went to Shem? What is bothering Rashi?

   Hint:

Look at the *dibbur hamaschil.*

YOUR ANSWER:

WHAT IS BOTHERING RASHI?

An Answer: Note the *dibbur hamaschil* here: "She went to inquire..." If Rebecca prayed to G-d, the word ותלך is inappropriate. To speak to G-d one need not go anywhere, since He is omnipresent; the whole world is filled with His glory. What, then, does the word ותלך mean here?

How does Rashi deal with this?

RASHI'S ANSWER

Rashi thus concludes that "she went to inquire of G-d" somewhere. Where would she go if she wanted to seek out G-d? To a man of G-d. Rashi's choice of Shem (instead of, for example, Abraham) is probably based on the Torah's choice of the word לדרוש, which is somewhat unusual. The Beis Medrash of Shem was known to have existed at that time. The verbal association between לדרוש and בית מדרש supplies the connection between Rebecca's seeking G-d and her going to the prophet Shem.

This *drash* is considered by many *p'shat*-oriented commentators to be *p'shat*, precisely because the words ותלך לדרוש demand it.

(See Devek Tov)

❖ ❖ ❖

Rashi offers two commentaries stemming from two bases for p'shat in-terpretations.

Genesis 25:28

ויאהב יצחק את עשו כי ציד בפיו ורבקה אהבת את יעקב.

> **בפיו:** כתרגומו, בפיו של יצחק. ומדרשו בפיו של עשיו שהיה צד אותו ומרמהו בדבריו.
>
> **[There was prey] in his mouth:** *Rashi:* Understand this as the Targum renders it — in Isaac's mouth. But its midrashic explanation is: in Esau's mouth, meaning he [Esau] used to entrap and deceive him [Isaac] by his words.

The question here should be obvious. What is it?

YOUR QUESTION:

QUESTIONING RASHI

An Answer: Rashi's first explanation would appear to be the *p'shat*. Why the need for the midrashic interpretation?

What Is Bothering Rashi?

Remember we had said that when Rashi offers two interpretations, it is assumed that the first one is weak in some way. The second also has a weakness, otherwise Rashi would have brought it as the only comment. What is bothering Rashi about the *p'shat* interpretation?

Clue:

Look at the *dibbur hamaschil* carefully. How do you understand it?

Your Answer:

An Answer: The reference of the pronoun in the word בפיו, "in his mouth," is unclear; in whose mouth? Isaac's or Esau's? The simple *p'shat* would say it is Isaac's (i.e., Isaac ate with his mouth) the prey that Esau hunted. This would seem to be the thrust of the whole story. The total context supports this interpretation, and this is Rashi's first explanation. But there is a problem. A pronoun usually refers back to the last noun (name) mentioned; here the last name is Esau. It would therefore seem to refer to Esau's mouth and not Isaac's.

Analyzing Rashi's Comment

There is another difficulty with the first explanation. Can you find it? Look closely at the text (in the Hebrew, of course).

Your Answer:

An Answer: The text literally says "because ציד in his mouth." If the word בפיו refers to Isaac's mouth, then the sentence reads: "because he [Esau] put prey in his [Isaac's] mouth." But there is a problem with this reading. The verb "to put" or "to give" is missing. The Torah should have said: "He *put* prey in his mouth." The midrash is hinting that since the verb "to put" is absent, then we have to construct a sentence that does not need the words "to put." We can do this if Isaac himself is the prey. The sentence would then read: "because he [Isaac] was prey in his [Esau's] mouth." This avoids the need to artificially insert the words "he put" in the sentence. The meaning then is: Isaac was captured and captivated by his son's deceptions. Esau deceived his father, Isaac, who was easy prey.

THE MIDRASHIC INTERPRETATION

Thus the midrashic interpretation avoids the two difficulties mentioned above:

1) A pronoun usually refers back to the last-mentioned person. In this interpretation it does — it refers back to Esau.

2) The mystery of the missing noun ("to put"). Nothing is missing in the midrashic interpretation. Isaac was the prey (ציד) in Esau's mouth.

(See Ramban; Be'er Yitzchak)

❖ ❖ ❖

This comment has given the supercommentaries a lot of trouble, because it is difficult to make out Rashi's intent. In fact, his precise use of language is brilliantly illustrated in this comment.

Genesis 26:18

וישב יצחק ויחפר את בארת המים אשר חפרו בימי אברהם אביו ויסתמום פלשתים אחרי מות אברהם ויקרא להן שמות כשמות אשר קרא להן אביו.

וישב ויחפר: הבארות אשר חפרו בימי אברהם אביו ופלשתים סתמום מקודם שנסע יצחק מגרר חזר וחפרן.

And he dug again: *Rashi:* Those wells which they had dug in the days of Abraham his father and which the Philistines had stopped up, before Isaac left Gerar he dug them again.

Certainly Rashi comes to tell us something. But what?

YOUR QUESTION:

QUESTIONING RASHI

Rashi appears to be saying the same words as the Torah. What is he telling us?

---

*Rashi text according to Chavel edition.

What is bothering him?

Look closely.

YOUR ANSWER:

What Is Bothering Rashi?

An Answer: This one is not easy. We must look closely at Rashi's every word. At first glance it looks like he is quoting the sentence nearly verbatim. Note the sentence in the Torah: "And Isaac dug again the wells of water which they had dug in the days of Abraham his father and the Philistines stopped them up after the death of Abraham . . ." Compare this with what Rashi says. Is there any difference between the two?

Look closely.

YOUR ANSWER:

Analyzing Rashi

Our job in analyzing Rashi here is to note the subtle differences between what he says and what the Torah says. This should lead us to Rashi's message. We must understand both what Rashi is saying and why he needs to say it.

We have a clue. We have said that when Rashi quotes a verse in the body of his commentary but adds a word or two (he does here),he is usually warning us about a potential misunderstanding of the sentence's meaning (type II comment).

Can you make out what Rashi is telling us?

YOUR ANSWER:

Understanding Rashi

The one clear addition that Rashi makes to the text are his words "before Isaac left Gerar he dug them again." Rashi is telling us that Isaac dug these wells before he left Gerar. Now compare the Torah text, sentences 15–18. Sentence 17 says that Isaac left Gerar and encamped in the Valley of Gerar. Sentence 18 says: "And Isaac again dug (וישב ויחפור) wells, etc." The

Torah seems to say that Isaac dug the wells after he left the city of Gerar. Rashi says the opposite. Why?

Hint:

Look for another slight emendation that Rashi makes.

YOUR ANSWER:

An Answer: Knowledge of Biblical Hebrew helps here. Look at Rashi closely. Note another subtle change he makes in the wording. He writes ופלשתים סתמום, while the Torah says ויסתמום פלשתים. This change of word order means that the Philistines *had* stopped them up (pluperfect), not "the Philistines stopped them up." The meaning is that the Philistines had already stopped them up before the previous event — before Isaac left Gerar (sentence 17). So Rashi is telling us that the order of events as described in these sentences is not as would first appear. We might have thought that Abraham dug wells, then he died, then the Philistines stopped them up, then Isaac left Gerar, then he returned to redig them.

Rashi tells us that the correct order is: The wells were stopped up after Abraham's death, then Isaac redug them and then he moved from Gerar. They were never stopped up after that.

A CLOSER LOOK

By this time you may have noted another unclarity in the Torah's words that Rashi is dealing with here. I believe that the following explanation is the real purpose for Rashi's comment. Let us look at it closely.

The Torah says וישב ויחפור. The word וישב can have two possible meanings.

What are they?

YOUR ANSWER:

An Answer: It can mean either

1. He dug again, or

2. He returned and dug.

Which one did Rashi choose? How do you know?

Your Answer:

Answer:

Understanding Rashi _____

The word can mean "and he returned," implying that after Isaac left Gerar he then returned to dig up the wells. But Rashi rejects this interpretation. He says the word וישב means "to do again" — here "to dig again." Since Isaac did the digging before he left Gerar, he had no need to return there. Rather, while still in Gerar, "he redug the wells of water that they dug in the days of Abraham." This is what he means when he says מקודם שנסע יצחק מגרר חזר וחפרן, meaning "before he left Gerar he redug (חזר וחפרן) them." By substituting the word חזר for the Torah's word וישב, Rashi is telling us that the word means "to do again" and not "to return."

This difficult Rashi shows how he subtly realigns the Torah's words to give us a more correct understanding of them. In so doing he helps us avoid a most likely misunderstanding.

(See Mizrachi)

Close analysis of Rashi's comment reveals an original interpretation, which he considers to be p'shat.

Genesis: 27:28

ויתן לך האלקים מטל השמים ומשמני הארץ ורב דגן ותירש.

> **ויתן לך:** ויחזור ויתן. ולפי פשוטו מוסב לענין ראשון: ראה ריח בני,
> שנתן לו הקב"ה, כריח שדה וגו' ועוד יתן לך מטל השמים וגו'.
> **And may He give you:** *Rashi:* May He give and repeat and give again. However, according to its simple meaning it refers back to the preceding topic: "See the fragrance of my son, which the Holy One Blessed Be He, has given him, is like the fragrance of a field, etc. And may He also give you the dew of the heavens, etc."

Rashi gives two interpretations — one he calls *p'shat* and one not.

What would you ask here?

YOUR QUESTIONS:

QUESTIONING RASHI

Questions: First: What is bothering Rashi? Why must he offer any interpretations? Isn't the sentence clear as it stands? Look carefully at the *dibbur
hamaschil.*

Second: Why two interpretations?

Third: In the *p'shat* interpretation, Rashi quotes part of the previous
sentence, but he adds the words "which the Holy One Blessed Be He
has given him . . ." He certainly didn't add them for nothing, so why
did he add them?

YOUR ANSWER TO THE FIRST QUESTION:

WHAT IS BOTHERING RASHI?

An Answer: Most commentaries agree that Rashi is bothered by the fact that the
sentence begins with the word "And." This seems to imply that the
blessing here is not the first one mentioned, but an addition to one
previously mentioned. But no blessing is mentioned until now. It is
this difficulty that Rashi addresses.

How does Rashi answer this question?

YOUR ANSWER:

UNDERSTANDING RASHI

An Answer: Rashi reinterprets the word "And" in "And may [He] give you" to mean
"May He give AND give AND give, . . ." the word "and" being a poetic way to
signify continuance, an unending giving. But Rashi doesn't consider this
p'shat. Why?

YOUR ANSWER:

Answer: Perhaps simply because "and" means "and" and not "unending."

Now to our third question.

Why does Rashi add the words "which the Holy One Blessed Be He has given him, . . ." to the Torah's own words, in his second interpretation? (This looks like a Type II comment, meant to steer us clear of a misunderstanding.)

This is not easy.

Hint:

Reread the second half of sentence 27:27.

ויאמר ראה ריח בני כריח שדה אשר ברכו ה'.

"and he said: See the fragrance of my son is like the fragrance of a field which G-d has blessed."

What do the words אשר ברכו ה' — "which G-d has blessed," mean? What, or whom, did G-d bless?

YOUR ANSWER:

In-Depth Anaylsis _____

Answer: Rashi gives the previous sentence (27:27) an unusual interpretation (which he considers to be *p'shat*). At first glance the sentence seems to say "See the fragrance of my son is like the fragrance of a field which (= the field) G-d has blessed." In this reading it is the field that is blessed. But Rashi interprets these words differently. He says it is Jacob who is blessed with the fragrance. This is what Rashi means when he adds the words "the fragrance of my son, *which the Holy One, Blessed Be He, has given him . . .*" Rashi's addition tells us that Isaac says G-d blessed Jacob ("my son") by giving him a pleasant fragrance (and not the field). The new meaning is thus: G-d blessed Jacob by giving him a fragrance like the field. *And* may He also give [him] of the dew of the heavens etc.

We see how this explains the word "and" at the beginning of sentence 28. This is truly an original view of the Torah's words. Rashi considers this to be *p'shat*, probably, as we said, because in this interpretation the word "and" means "and"; it is not bent out of shape as it is in the first interpretation.

(See *Mizrachi*)

Once more a close reading of the Torah's words leads us to Rashi's interpretation based on a midrash.

Genesis 28:12

ויחלם והנה סלם מצב ארצה וראשו מגיע השמימה והנה מלאכי אלקים עלים וירדים בו.

עולים ווירדים: עולים תחלה ואח״כ יורדים מלאכים שליווהו בארץ אין יוציאם חוצה לארץ ועלו לרקיע וירדו מלאכי חוצה לארץ ללוותו.

Ascending and descending: *Rashi:* Ascending first and afterwards descending. Those angels who accompanied him in the Land [of Israel] were not permitted to leave the Land, they ascended to Heaven and angels from outside the Land descended to accompany him.

What is your question on this Rashi?

YOUR QUESTION:

QUESTIONING RASHI

A Question: This comment contains an interesting midrash — that Eretz Yisroel has its own guardian angels — but certainly this is not to be found in the the words of the Torah; this really cannot be considered *p'shat*. Why does Rashi feel the need to tell us this? What is bothering him?

Hint:

Look at the *dibbur hamaschil.*

YOUR ANSWER:

WHAT IS BOTHERING RASHI?

An Answer: The verse says, "And he dreamt and behold a ladder set up on earth and the top of it reached the heavens; and behold angels of G-d were ascending and descending it." Rashi is bothered by the order of the words — "ascending" before "descending." The natural habitat of angels is in the heavens; we would expect them first to descend from their place of residence and only afterwards to ascend back to it. How is that we have the angels ascending before they descended?

Rashi's comment is intended to answer this question. How does he?

YOUR ANSWER:

RASHI'S INTERPRETATION

Rashi clarifies this point and thus explains the angels' reverse ladder choreography. The ascending angels originated in Eretz Yisroel (not in Heaven, as we had assumed) and they accompanied Jacob on his way out — thus it is fitting that these angels ascended. The descending angels were from a different group, which were situated in the Heavens.

Can you find support in the Torah for this *drash*, for the fact that there are two sets of accompanying angels?

Hint:

Review the whole *parshah* in your search.

YOUR ANSWER:

SUPPORT FOR RASHI'S INTERPRETATION

An Answer: See the end of this *parshah* (Genesis 32:1-2). There it speaks of Jacob, on his return to Eretz Yisroel, meeting angels of G-d. See the Rashi on these two sentences. The midrash rounds out the whole *parshah* beautifully with the image of Jacob being protected in his trials and tribulations by G-d's ministering angels.

(See *Nachalas Ya'akov*)

 ❖ ❖ ❖

The following complex Rashi teaches us two lessons about his commentary.

1) *Considering Rashi's verbal economy, long comments have to be studied carefully for their full meaning.*

2) *Some comments can only be understood when they are seen in light of neighboring Rashi comments.*

Genesis 28:21

ושבתי בשלום אל בית אבי והיה הי לי לאלקים.

והיה הי לי לאלוקים: שיחול שמו עלי מתחלה ועד סוף שלא ימצא פסול בזרעי כמו שנאמר "אשר דברתי לך" והבטחה זו הבטיח לאברהם שנאמר "להיות לך לאלוקים ולזרעך אחריך"

And the L-rd will be a G-d to me: *Rashi:* That His Name shall rest upon me from the beginning to the end, that no unworthy person shall be found in my descendants — as it is said: אשר דברתי לך — "[Until I have done] that which I spoke concerning you" (28:15). And this promise He made to Abraham, as it says להיות לך לאלוקים ולזרעך אחריך. "To be a G-d unto you and unto your seed after you" (Genesis 17:7).

Rashi seems to be reading a lot into this *dibbur hamaschil*. In trying to make sense out of his comment we should ask:

YOUR QUESTION:

QUESTIONING RASHI

What is the relevance of what Rashi says to the Torah's words ?

What is bothering Rashi? And why is he stressing the matter of worthy descendants?

Can you see what is bothering Rashi?

YOUR ANSWER:

WHAT IS BOTHERING RASHI?

This is a complex comment and requires patience to understand. We will take it piece by piece to try to understand Rashi's intent.

Answer: Look at Jacob's vow (sentences 20–23), bearing in mind the *dibbur hamaschil*. What is strange about the words "And the L-rd will be a G-d to me"?

THINK . . .

Answer: At first reading it looks like Jacob is making a deal with G-d, namely, if G-d fulfills Jacob's conditions ("being with me, guarding me on the way, providing bread to eat, etc.") then Jacob will accept Him as his G-d! ("And the L-rd will be a G-d to me.") This is the height of presumptuousness! One does not make deals with G-d.

The whole of Rashi's comment is geared to answering this question — how could Jacob make conditions with G-d? This, then, is what is bothering Rashi. He is intent on finding the answer in the text itself.

Understanding Rashi

To fully understand this comment we have to see Rashi's comments on the previous sentences (20–21). There he draws a parallel between G-d's promise to Jacob and Jacob's vow. The parallelism, while clearly evident in the text, is often overlooked. Below we have it in outline form.

G-d's promise		*Jacob's vow*
הנה אנכי עמך בכל אשר תלך	←	אם יהיה אלקים עמדי
ושמרתיך בכל אשר תלך	←	שמרני בדרך הזה
כי לא אעזבך	←	ונתן לי לחם לאכל
השיבותיך אל האדמה הזאת	←	ושבתי בשלום אל בית אבי
?	←	והיה ה׳ לי לאלקים

The parallelism is remarkable. But there is a problem: Jacob's words והיה ה׳ לי לאלקים have no parallel in G-d's promise! For all other parts of Jacob's vow we find an identical or similar phrase in G-d's promise, but not for this phrase.

Can you find the parallel in G-d's promise?

Your Answer:

Rashi's Answer

Rashi says that the words אשר דברתי לך (28:15) in G-d's promise is parallel to the words והיה ה' לי לאלוקים in Jacob's vow. How? Note Rashi's step-by-step deduction.

1. "Which I spoke concerning (and not 'to') you," refers to G-d's promise to Abraham concerning his children, among them Jacob. See Rashi 28:15 where he shows that this phrase cannot mean "which I spoke to you," because G-d had never spoken to Jacob previously.

2. What had G-d promised Abraham then? "And I will establish My covenant between Me and you and your offspring after you, throughout their generations for a covenant forever, to be a G-d to you (להיות לך לאלוקים) and to your offspring after you."

See how this phrase in G-d's promise to Abraham is remarkably similar to והיה ה' לי לאלוקים in Jacob's vow.

This, then, is the missing phrase. And while this phrase was spoken to Abraham, it was spoken about Jacob (Abraham's offspring).

Now we see why Rashi makes reference to the offspring of Abraham. Note the words להיות לך לאלוקים ולזרעך אחריך. "To be a G-d to you and to your offspring AFTER YOU." G-d will only be the G-d of those of Abraham's offspring who go AFTER him! We now understand Rashi's stress on off-spring that have no unworthy person among them. Only those who "go after" Abraham are worthy of this covenant and promise.

Summarizing Rashi

In summary: Rashi shows, by means of close textual analysis and comparison, how Jacob's words are not meant to cut a deal with G-d but rather are an expression of his wish that he and his children be worthy of being chosen by G-d. We see how every facet of this comment is necessary. By clearly developing his thought, Rashi has answered the questions that should have bothered us:

1. The words והיה ה' לי לאלוקים are not a condition that Jacob demands of G-d; it is, rather, Jacob's repetition of G-d's promise to him.

2. That phrase too, as every other part of Jacob's vow, has its parallel in G-d's promise in the words אשר דברתי לך.

An Even Closer Look _____

Rashi uses the strange phrase שיחול שמו עלי מתחלה ועד סוף — "that His Name will rest on me from the beginning to end."

What does he mean by "from the beginning to end" ?

YOUR ANSWER:

An Answer: One interpretation is that Jacob's offspring should not be like Abraham's son Yishmael who, while evil most of his life, repented at the end of his life. And not like Isaac's son Esau, who, from the beginning of his life until age 13, was righteous but then strayed. Jacob asked for offspring who would be righteous from the beginning of their life to the end of their life.

(See *Mizrachi*)

In this comment there are both Type I and Type II comments. Can you find them?

Genesis 30:30

כי מעט אשר היה לך לפני ויפרץ לרב ויברך הי אתך לרגלי ועתה
מתי אעשה גם אנכי לביתי.

> **גם אנכי לביתי**: לצורך ביתי, עכשיו אין עושים לצרכי אלא בני,
> וצריך אני להיות עושה גם אני עמהם לסמכן. וזהו גם.
>
> **Also I, for my household:** *Rashi:* For the needs of my household. At present my sons alone provide for my needs, but I, also, ought to provide together with them, to assist them. That is [the meaning of] "also."

Rashi seems to be saying two separate things:

1. For the needs of my household

2. In addition to my sons, I also should provide for my house.

What would you ask about these statements?

YOUR QUESTIONS:

Questioning Rashi _____

Questions: One question: Why does Rashi say "for the needs of my house" and not simply "for my house," as the verse has it ?

A second question: Why does Rashi bring the issue of Jacob's sons providing for his household?

What is disturbing him?

Think . . .

Clue:

Look at the words in the *dibbur hamaschil.*

Your Answer:

What Is Bothering Rashi? _____

Answer: Let's take the second question first. Rashi is concerned with the location of the word גם, "also," in this sentence.

What is problematic with this word here?

Think . . .

Your answer:

Answer: Until now Jacob has worked exclusively for Laban. He now makes a plea for starting to work for his own family. In that case, the sentence should have read: מתי אעשה אנכי גם לביתי — "When will *I provide also for my own household*?" Meaning: I have provided for you, now it is time to provide also for myself. And not as the verse states: מתי אעשה גם אנכי לביתי. "When will *also I provide* for my household?" This phrasing implies that someone is already providing for his household, and now Jacob also wants to provide for them.

How does Rashi's comment deal with this problem?

Rashi explains the use of גם in a slightly different way.

How?

Your Answer:

UNDERSTANDING RASHI

Answer: Rashi concedes that the unusual implication of the sentence is, in fact, the correct one. Someone else had been providing for his family until now — his sons. Now, Jacob says, he also wants to help them provide.

He ends by saying: This is the use of the word "also" here. These last words of Rashi show us clearly that the meaning of the word גם was bothering him.

WHAT ELSE IS BOTHERING RASHI?

Let us return to the first question we had. Why the use of "The needs of my house" instead of "for my house," as the Torah itself says?

Do you have an explanation?

RASHI HELPS US AVOID A MISUNDERSTANDING

An answer: Rashi is clarifying matters here (a typical Type II comment). We might have thought that "for my household" was meant literally, implying that Jacob wanted now to stop working for Laban and begin working "for [his] household." But that was not Jacob's intent, for we see that , in fact, he continued to work for Laban. Therefore, the literal "for my household" cannot be the meaning. It must, rather, mean, that the wages Jacob will earn for his work for Laban would go "for the needs" of his own family.

A CLOSER LOOK

It is interesting to note that the Ramban takes Rashi to task on this point. He disagrees with Rashi's interpretation, both on grammatical and common-sense grounds. Jacob's children were young, the oldest being just six years old! How could they be the providers of his household? As far as the syntax goes, says the Ramban, we have other examples in the Torah where the word גם is placed awkwardly, yet it retains its common-sense meaning. Here, too, its meaning is, as we would have expected, "when will I provide also for my family and not just for your family," notwithstanding its location in the sentence.

IN RASHI'S DEFENSE

How would you defend Rashi?

(See Mizrachi)

In this Rashi comment we see different approaches to understanding Rashi's intent.

Genesis 31:39

טרפה לא הבאתי אליך אנכי אחטנה מידי תבקשנה גנבתי יום וגנבתי
לילה.

טרפה: על ידי ארי וזאב.

That which was mangled : *Rashi:* By a lion or a wolf.

What would you ask here?

Questioning Rashi

An obvious question is:

Why does Rashi specify these animals? And if Laban's sheep were ripped to shreds by another animal, would not Jacob have to protect them or pay for them?

And in addition we could ask: What is wrong with the statement as it is?

Jacob says, "I was very responsible, I always paid for any damages, even when the sheep were ripped apart." Why must Rashi offer any comment here?

What Is Bothering Rashi?

Your Answer:

An Answer: Rashi is possibly bothered by Jacob's taking pride in fulfilling his basic responsibility. He was a shepherd, after all; it was his job to protect these sheep. If he failed, why should he not be held responsible? Why is he so proud that he did what was expected of him?

How does Rashi deal with this question?

Hint:

See Exodus 22:12.

Your Answer:

Understanding Rashi

Answer: That hint was the answer! There it says "the torn one (הטרפה) he shall not pay."

81 —

And Rashi on that verse says that sometimes he does pay and sometimes he does not. If it was torn by a vicious animal, a lion or wolf, then he does not have to pay.

This, then, is Jacob's pride: Even when, according to the law, he would be exempt, Jacob nevertheless paid for the loss. So Laban never lost anything during Jacob's shepherding.

ANOTHER VIEW

It is interesting to note that the *Sefer Zikaron*, an early and famous supercommentator on Rashi, rejects this explanation. He says Laban the Aramite could not possibly have cared about Jewish Halachah. This may be clever *pilpul*, but it cannot be the meaning in this verse.

He suggests something simpler. The word טרפה can have two meanings. Either:

1) mortally ill (for example, lung damage) or

2) ripped by another animal.

Rashi's comment tells us that the first meaning is not appropriate here.

Can you suggest why?

YOUR ANSWER:

Answer: Jacob could never have prevented such internal illnesses; neither is he due any praise if they did not become טרפה. Thus Rashi tells us that טרפה means torn apart. The fact that Rashi chose "lion or wolf" is, in his view, inconsequential.

The *Sefer Zikaron* is known for his straighforward approach. We see here that he is not satisfied with a clever answer, as long as he does not think it is the true answer.

(See *Nachalas Ya'akov*)

פרשת וישלח

This comment indicates that Rashi's preference for p'shat over drash does not preclude the choice of a supernatural over a natural explanation.

Genesis: 32:3

וישלח יעקב מלאכים לפניו אל עשו אחיו ארצה שעיר שדה אדום.

וישלח יעקב מלאכים: מלאכים ממש.

And Jacob sent messengers: *Rashi:* Angels literally.

What would you ask about this brief comment?

YOUR QUESTION:

QUESTIONING RASHI

Answer: This is a one-word comment, a Type II comment. The usual question, "What is bothering Rashi?" is not appropriate. What question is appropriate?

YOUR ANSWER:

FROM WHAT MISUNDERSTANDING IS RASHI GUARDING US?

Answer: Rashi has chosen to translate the word מלאכים as "angels" and not simply as "messengers." He is telling us that, though we might have thought so, these are not human messengers.

Why would he abandon the more natural-likelihood that these were human messengers and opt for the less-likely interpretation that these were angels?

What leads him to this conclusion?

Hint:

See the total context of this sentence.

YOUR ANSWER:

UNDERSTANDING RASHI _____

An Answer: Rashi bases his comment on the fact that immediately before this sentence we are told that Jacob met מלאכי אלוקים, "Angels of G-d." Therefore, by means of textual comparison, Rashi concludes that the word מלאכים here also means angels of G-d. In the Torah we find both human messengers as well as G-dly messengers referred to as מלאכים. Rashi chose the one most appropriate to the context.

(See Mesiach Ilmim)

❖ ❖ ❖

Rashi is always sensitive to apparent redundancies. His comment shows the unique meaning of each word.

Genesis 32:7

ויירא יעקב מאד ויצר לו ויחץ את העם אשר אתו ואת הצאן ואת הבקר והגמלים לשני מחנות.

ויירא ויצר: ויירא שמא יהרג,ויצר לו אם יהרוג הוא את אחרים.
He feared and was distressed: *Rashi:* He was afraid lest he be killed and he was distressed that he might have to kill someone.

What can you ask here?

YOUR QUESTION:

QUESTIONING RASHI: _____

Question: What provoked Rashi to suggest that Jacob was afraid of these two different fears?

YOURV ANSWER:

What Is Bothering Rashi?

An Answer: Rashi notes the redundancy of the two terms, "He feared" and "he was distressed."

Rashi, as opposed to some other commentators (e.g., the Radak), does not allow for literary redundancies in the Torah just for the sake of emphasis. If the same idea is repeated in different words, then each word must be understood to convey its own meaning. Actually, a very similar argument is found in the Talmud itself (*Sanhedrin* 64b). There, we find Rabbi Akiva and Rabbi Yishmael taking opposite stands on redundancies in the Torah. Rabbi Akiva says each word has its own message, while Rabbi Yishmael says, "The Torah speaks in the language of men," meaning that redundancies are normally used to emphasize a point and not to make fine distinctions between different meanings. Rashi appears to lean toward Rabbi Akiva's view.

Understanding Rashi

In our verse, we see that Rashi attaches two separate, but related, meanings to the two terms. Thus, they are not redundant; they each tell us something about Jacob's fears.

A Closer Look

It is clear that Jacob feared being killed by his brother Esau. But what evidence do we have that he was also "distressed" that he might kill someone?

Hint:

Find another Rashi comment that supports this:

YOUR ANSWER:

An Answer: The sentence continues to tell us that Jacob split up his group into two camps. Then we are told, "And he said: If Esau come to the one camp and smite it then the remaining camp will escape." On this verse Rashi comments: "In spite of him, for I will fight against him." So we see that Jacob was getting ready to kill or be killed.

Both possibilities distressed him. We have Jacob fearing both the bodily fear of being killed and the moral fear of having to kill another human being, even if the victim is his mortal enemy. We saw a similar sensitivity with Abraham (above, Genesis 15:1).

A Deeper Look

Why does Rashi associate the fear of being killed with the word וירא while he associates the fear of killing another with the word ויצר לו.

YOUR ANSWER:

An Answer: The word ירא, "fear," usually means fear of bodily or personal harm (see Genesis 18:15, 26:7, 31:31), while the word ויצר is also used for emotional pain (see Samuel II, 1:26). It is interesting to note that the word "anxiety" in English is derived from the Latin "anxius" meaning "to choke" — that is, the constriction one feels in one's throat when nervous. In Hebrew the root צר means narrow or constricted, as well. This may be why this word is associated with psychological distress, the kind Jacob would feel were he to kill someone.

(See *Bereishis Rabbah*)

❖ ❖ ❖

This very brief Rashi clarifies a point by a subtle switch in word order.

Genesis 32:16

גמלים מיניקות ובניהם שלשים פרות ארבעים ופרים עשרה אתנת עשרים ועירם עשרה.

גמלים מיניקות: שלושים ובניהם עמהם.
Nursing camels: *Rashi:* THIRTY AND THEIR COLTS with them.

Look at this comment carefully.

What is your question?

Questioning Rashi

What has Rashi told us here? If he is telling us that the colts were with the camels, that is stated explicitly in the sentence itself. What, then, is he adding?

Remember our rule: If a Rashi comment consists of adding a word or two to the words of the Torah or changing their order, then it is likely that Rashi intends to help us avoid a posssible misunderstanding.

From What Misunderstanding Is Rashi Guarding Us? _____

Hint:

Notice carefully what Rashi does here. How does he arrange the words of the sentence? Why does he rearrange them?

Your Answer:

An Answer: Rashi senses a confusion in the words of this sentence. The problem is more pronounced in the Hebrew. It reads: "Nursing camels and their colts, thirty; forty cows, etc. . ."

Now ask yourself: How many camels were there in this group? Were there thirty altogether with their colts? or were there thirty camels in addition to their colts? It is not clear. The Torah text seems to say that there were thirty altogether, for it says literally: "Nursing camels and their colts = thirty."

What do you say — how many were there?

Your Answer:

Understanding Rashi _____

An Answer: Rashi warns us against the interpretation that there were thirty altogether. According to him, there were "Thirty camels plus their colts with them." Rashi tells us this by a slight rearrangement of the words. The Torah has: גמלים מניקות ובניהם שלושים while Rashi has: גמלים מניקות ובניהם שלשים עמהם. Rashi's rearrangement of the words here is so subtle that it is usually overlooked.

But we must ask: How does Rashi know that this, in fact, is the correct interpretation?

What support can you find for his interpretation?

Think . . .

Look at sentences 14 and 15.

Your Answer:

Support for Rashi's Interpretation

An Answer: If we look carefully, we see that the animals are listed in descending numerical order:

> two hundred she-goats and twenty he-goats (200 + 20);
>
> two hundred ewes and twenty rams (200 + 20);
>
> [thirty camels];
>
> forty cows and tens bulls (40 + 10) ;
>
> twenty she-donkeys and ten he-donkeys (20 + 10).

If the list is in descending order and if there are a total of only thirty camels, then the camels are out of place, for they are less than the fifty cattle that follow them in the list. It is for this reason that Rashi surmises that there were thirty camels plus their colts, making the number almost certainly more than fifty and probably at least sixty (one colt for each mother). In that case, the camels are placed in the correct descending order.

> 220 goats
>
> 220 sheep
>
> 50-60 camels
>
> 50 cattle
>
> 30 asses

Note: Some Chumashim with Rashi are not sensitive to the significance of this slight switch in word order, and they have an incorrect quote of Rashi's comment.

(See Mesiach Ilmim)

Following is an example of Rashi's using the Aramaic Targum Onkelos.

Genesis 34:31

ויאמרו הכזונה יעשה את אחותנו.

> **את אחותנו:** ית אחתנא.
> **Our sister:** *Rashi:* Our sister (in Aramaic, as the Targum).

What can you ask here?

YOUR QUESTION:

QUESTIONING RASHI

Rashi simply translates the Hebrew into Aramaic. The obvious question is:

What is he telling us? and why?

WHAT IS RASHI TELLING US?

YOUR ANSWER:

An Answer: To understand what Rashi is telling us, you must understand Biblical Hebrew. The sentence, as it stands, could be translated in one of two ways. Rashi is telling us which of the two is correct.

What are the two ways this *dibbur hamaschil* can be translated?

YOUR ANSWER:

1)

2)

WHAT IS BOTHERING RASHI ?

Answer: The Hebrew word את can either:

1) Mean "with" as in: Genesis 37:2

אלה תולדות יעקב יוסף בן שבע עשרה שנה היה רעה **את** אחיו בצאן והוא נער **את** בני בלהה ו**את** בני זלפה נשי אביו וגו׳.

These are the offspring of Jacob: Joseph, being seventeen years old, was feeding the flock **with** his brothers, and the lad was **with** the sons of Bilhah and **with** the sons of Zilpah, his father's wives, etc.

Here we see in one sentence the use of את meaning "with." And note that the Targum is עם in each case.

In our sentence this would mean: "Should he act *with* our sister as with a harlot?"

2) Or it can be used before a direct object, thus having no translation in English. As in:

Genesis 1:1

בראשית ברא אלוקים **את** השמים **ואת** הארץ.

"In the beginning G-d created (את) the Heavens and (את) the Earth."

Note the Targum here has ית each time.

In our sentence this would mean: "Should he make our sister as a harlot?"

By citing Onkelos, Rashi clarifies that the correct choice is #2. As we saw, the Targum makes the meaning clear, since there are two different Aramaic words for the Hebrew את. When used to mean "with," he translates the word as עם. When used before a direct object, he translates it as ית. By using ית here, the meaning becomes "Should he make our sister as a harlot?"

Why does Rashi choose this translation? Find support in common sense.

YOUR ANSWER:

UNDERSTANDING RASHI

An Answer: Dinah was abducted, taken forcibly by Shechem. She certainly didn't act like a harlot, soliciting customers. She was not "with" Shechem willingly. He took her body but not her will. To say that he "would do *with* her as with a harlot" would give the false impression that Dinah consented. Rashi understandably rejects this option and clarifies the point by quoting the Targum Onkelos.

Rashi and Onkelos: An Additional Note

Some Rashi commentators claim that Rashi's only intent here is to clarify the correct wording in the Targum text because there are variant versions. One version is יעבד ית אחתנא — "will make our sister," which seems to be the one that Rashi had. Another one is יתעבד לאחתנא — "will be done to our sister." Perhaps Rashi rejects the latter as an incorrect translation of the Hebrew. In either case, the basic meaning is the same. Both mean: "will be done *to* our sister." Whether or not this is Rashi's purpose in his comment here, it is true that at times he will cite the Targum in order to set straight the correct text in the Targum.

In his Torah commentary, Rashi refers to the Targum in various ways. He may simply say כתרגומו, which directs the student to see how Onkelos translates the word or phrase. He may do this to clarify a grammatical point or to get a correct translation of a difficult Hebrew word, or he may want to point out a midrash which the Targum cites. Rashi may quote the Targum in addition to his own *p'shat*, then he will introduce it with the words ואונקלוס תרגם. And sometimes Rashi will quote the Aramaic without mentioning Onkelos (as in our case), though the quote does come from Onkelos.

(See *Be'er BaSadeh*)

This Rashi is a tongue-twister and a brain-teaser! To understand it, we must realize the problem in the text. Then we must figure out how Rashi goes about solving it. From this comment we can also learn something about Rashi's terminology.

Genesis: 37:18

ויראו אתו מרחק ובטרם יקרב אליהם ויתנכלו אתו להמיתו.

ויתנכלו: נתמלאו נכלים וערמומיות.

אתו: כמו אתו, עמו כלומר אליו.

And they conspired: *Rashi:* They became filled with schemes and craftiness.

Against him: *Rashi:* The same as אתו, "with him," עמו, "with him" meaning אליו, "towards him."

QUESTIONING RASHI?

What is peculiar in this comment is more pronounced in the Hebrew, where Rashi moves from אותו (him) to אתו (with him) to עמו (with him) to אליו (towards him).

Why these verbal acrobatics? What is bothering Rashi?

Hint:

See Rashi's first comment on the word ויתנכלו.

YOUR ANSWER:

WHAT IS BOTHERING RASHI?

Answer: Knowledge of Hebrew grammar is essential to deciphering this comment.

The first word, ויתנכלו, is in the intransitive construction, meaning that the verb is reflexive (its object is the person himself, not someone or something else). See that Rashi says,"They became filled with schemes . . ." and not "They schemed against . . ."

In light of this first comment, the word אותו is inappropriate. Since the word means "him," it would translate literally as: "And they were filled with schemes him." It makes as little sense in Hebrew as it does in English.

How does Rashi deal with this problem?

YOUR ANSWER:

UNDERSTANDING RASHI

Answer: Step by step, Rashi shows how אותו means "towards him." The word אותו is sometimes, though not often, used to mean אתו, "with him" (see, for example, II Kings 3:12). And the word אתו more frequently has the meaning like עמו, "with him" (see Genesis 17:27). Now עמו always means "with him." But they weren't filled with schemes *with* him, as if to say that the brothers and Joseph conspired together. Certainly not. So Rashi's last associative step is that עמו is similar to אליו, "towards him."

Unfortunately, there is no biblical example of this אליו = עמו equation, therefore Rashi says "that is to say." But the logic is there. It is like saying, "They were preoccupied with him." Even though "preoccupied" is an intransitive verb, it makes sense to use it with the words "with him."

A DEEPER LOOK

One more question needs to be asked: Why didn't Rashi immediately translate the word אותו to mean אליו, "towards him"? Why the need for all the intermediary words?

Think . . .You should be able to figure it out.

YOUR ANSWER:

An answer: Rashi needed to approach the final translation by steps, for while each word is similar to the one preceding it, it is not similar to the word two steps away. That is, אותו is similar to אתו but not to עמו; likewise עמו is similar to אליו but not to אותו.

(See Havanas HaMikra)

A subtlety in the text alerts Rashi to a deeper meaning — and leads to a beautiful interpretation.

Genesis: 38:25

הוא מוצאת והיא שלחה אל חמיה לאמר לאיש אשר אלה לו אנכי הרה ותאמר הכר נא למי החתמת והפתילים והמטה האלה.

הכר נא: אין נא אלא לשון בקשה, הכר נא בוראך ואל תאבד שלוש נפשות.

Please recognize: *Rashi:* The word נא is nothing but an expression of request — I beg you, please recognize your Creator (be honest) and don't destroy three souls.

YOUR QUESTION:

QUESTIONING RASHI

Why this strange and seemingly forced interpretation? Why turn Tamar's clear request to Judah that he recognize the objects, into a plea that he recognize his Creator? What is bothering Rashi?

YOUR ANSWER:

WHAT IS BOTHERING RASHI?

An Answer: Rashi says clearly that the word נא means "Please," but in this case that is not appropriate. Tamar shows the objects to Judah, either he can or cannot recognize them. It is not a matter of will, where a request, נא, would be appropriate; it is a matter of ability and therefore "please" is inappropriate. This is what is bothering Rashi.

How is Rashi's comment an answer?

YOUR ANSWER:

UNDERSTANDING RASHI

An Answer: We can assume that Rashi reasoned as follows: Theoretically, Judah is either able or unable to recognize the objects, therefore the word "please'" is out of place here. But Tamar knew the truth and she knew quite well that he did recognize them. Her only question was: would he admit to it? She also realized that nothing could force Judah to admit the embarrassing truth. It was his word against hers. He was in the position of power and credibility. The only thing that would bring him to tell the truth was his conscience, his realization that his Creator knew the truth. He could fool everyone, but not G-d. She pleaded that he recognize his Creator and tell the truth.

A Deeper Look

Notice that Rashi (actually the midrash on which his comment is based) refers to G-d here as the Creator. Why?

Your Answer:

Answer: G-d has many names, and throughout his commentary Rashi uses various terms to refer to Him. He has used such names as the Holy One Blessed Be He, the Place, and, of course, the names used in the Torah. Here, for some reason, he chooses the term "the Creator." This recalls the Talmudic thought (*Kiddushin* 30b) that there are three partners in the creation of an individual — the Holy One Blessed Be He, his father and his mother. Tamar reminds Judah of the Creator, Who was instrumental in his own creation; so too should he be mindful not to destroy Tamar and those souls in her womb to whose creation he was partner. Truly a beautiful thought, one that could not but move Judah to confess.

(See Nachalas Yaakov)

This Rashi looks simple. But, as usual, the simplicity is deceptive. It is an excellent example of Rashi's style of reworking the text to clarify matters.

Genesis: 38:28–30

ויהי בלידתה ויתן יד ותקח המילדת ותקשר על ידו שני לאמר זה יצא ראשנה. ויהי כמשיב ידו והנה יצא אחיו ותאמר מה פרצת עליך פרץ ויקרא שמו פרץ. ואחר יצא אחיו אשר על-ידו השני ויקרא שמו זרח.

ויתן יד: הוציא האחד ידו לחוץ ולאחר שקשרה על ידו השני החזירה.

And he gave a hand: *Rashi:* The one extended his hand outside and after she bound unto his hand the scarlet thread, he returned it.

Read the comment carefully and clarify to yourself what it means. Then ask your question.

YOUR QUESTION:

QUESTIONING RASHI

What does Rashi tell us that we don't already know from the Torah text itself? He seems to be repeating what the Torah says in his own words.

WHAT IS BOTHERING RASHI HERE?

Clue:

What type of Rashi comment is this?

This looks like a Type II Comment. He seems to be rephrasing the sentence in his own words. Why? Is he warning us against a possible misunderstanding here?

YOUR ANSWER:

Clue #2:

Look closely at the comment and see what changes Rashi makes in the verse.

A Close Look at Rashi's Reworking of the Torah's Words_____

1. He replaces ויתן with the words הוציא לחוץ.

2. He inserts the word האחד, "the one."

3. He replaces the words ותקשור על ידו השני with ולאחר שקשרה על ידו
   החזירה.

Why has he done all this?

Your Answer:

What Is the Possible Misunderstanding? _____

Hint:

Reread all three sentences above (28–30).

What are these verses saying? Which baby came out first?

Your Answer:

The Possible Misunderstanding _____

The verses are misleading for several reasons:

1. The sequence of the first sentence seems to be saying that the one who gave a hand was already outside the womb. ("And it was when *she gave birth* that he gave a hand . . .") This impression is strengthened by the midwife's "This one went out first."

2. Yet the following two sentences seem to contradict this: "And it was when he returned his hand." We ask: Returned to where? We must now assume: to the womb. This then strongly implies that this baby was still in the womb. And then it tells us of the first real birth: "and behold his brother came out . . ."

3. Rashi's *dibbur hamaschil* is "And he gave a hand. "Giving" implies intentionality. Did the baby intentionally give his hand? Does that make sense?

4. Also, since it doesn't say "his hand," only "hand," it might be thought that someone nearby intentionally "gave a hand" to help the birth.

How does Rashi deal with these problems?

YOUR ANSWER:

UNDERSTANDING RASHI

These misunderstandings are dealt with by Rashi's emendations.

1. By changing ויתן to הוציא לחוץ, "he stretched outside," we see that only the hand was extended outside the womb. We also understand that "giving" here implies "extending" and not "intentionality."

2. By inserting the word האחד, "the one," we see that it was one of the babies that extended his hand, and not a bystander.

3. By adding לאחר שקשרה . . . החזירה "after she tied . . . he returned it," Rashi reinforces his point: the the baby was still in the womb and "his returning it" meant pulling the hand back into the womb. The words in the next sentence, "And it was when he drew his hand back . . .," do not mean that he just "drew his hand back" but rather that he "returned" it to the womb.

This comment is an example of Rashi's masterly reworking the text with minimal changes to help the student avoid a possible misreading of the Torah's words.

(see Mizrachi)

Rashi's comment transforms an abstract concept into its concrete expression. In doing so, a remarkable consistency in Joseph's character is revealed.

Genesis 39:3

וירא אדניו כי הי אתו וכל אשר הוא עשה הי מצליח בידו.

כי הי אתו: שם שמים שגור בפיו.
That the L-rd was with him: *Rashi:* The name of G-d was familiar in his mouth.

What can you ask on this Rashi?

YOUR QUESTION:

Questioning Rashi

Answer: Why doesn't Rashi take the sentence at face value, viz., that Joseph prospered in all his endeavors and that is evidence that G-d was with him?

What is bothering Rashi that brought him to interpret the sentence in this way?

Hint:

Read the whole sentence in the Chumash. Find an answer from your common sense.

Your Answer:

What Is Bothering Rashi?

Answer: It says: "And his master saw that the L-rd was with him." How could the Egyptian pagan Potiphar "see" that G-d was with Joseph? Joseph's success alone would not necessarily indicate that "G-d was with him." Material success can be explained in many other ways. Was Potiphar a prophet? Was he even a believer in G-d? Of course not.

How, then, did he see that G-d was with Joseph?

Your Answer:

Understanding Rashi

Answer: Because Joseph told him so! Whenever Joseph prospered at an endeavor, he said ברוך ה׳. He took no credit for himself, but, instead, he thanked G-d. Potiphar heard and made note of it. And he heard Joseph speak this way often. Because "The name of G-d was familiar in his mouth."

Can you find support for this?

Your Answer:

SUPPORT FOR RASHI'S INTERPRETATION

Answer: If we look through all the chapters, from here until the death of Joseph, we find an amazing thing: every time Joseph speaks, he mentions G-d's name. Well, practically every time. Count them.

See: Genesis 39:9; 40:8; 41:16; 41:25,28,32; 41:51; 42:18; 43:29; 45:5,7,8; 48:9; 50:19; 50:25.

G-d's name was certainly "familiar in his mouth!"

(See Mesiach Ilmim)

Here we see how each part of a Rashi-comment needs to be analyzed separately to be fully understood.

Genesis 41:7

ותבלענה השבלים הדקות את שבע השבלים הבריאות והמלאות וייקץ פרעה והנה חלום.

> **והנה חלום:** והנה נשלם חלום שלם לפניו והוצרך פותרים.
> **And behold it was a dream:** *Rashi:* And behold a whole dream was completed before him, and it needed interpreters.

As you look at this comment, what would you ask of Rashi?

YOUR QUESTION:

QUESTIONING RASHI

Question: Why the need for a comment here? The sentence seems clear enough — Pharaoh had a dream; we are told that he woke up and had had a dream.

What's bothering Rashi?

WHAT IS BOTHERING RASHI?

Hint:

Reread the section from the beginning.

Can you think of two questions?

YOUR QUESTIONS:

       1.

       2.

An Answer: Why are we told, "Behold it was a dream"? We surely know that! At the outset we are told, "And it came to pass at the end of two years that Pharaoh dreamed . . ." The statement must have another meaning, more than just informing us that Pharaoh had a dream. So our first question is

    1. Why does the Torah tell us, "Behold it was dream"?

Our second question is, if it was necessary to tell us it was a dream, then:

    2. Why weren't we told after Pharaoh's first dream (41:4), "Behold it was a dream"?

These questions prompt Rashi to give his interpretation to these simple words.

Can you understand how Rashi's comment deals with these questions?

YOUR ANSWER:

UNDERSTANDING RASHI

The word והנה, "And behold," conveys a sense of realization, not just a statement of fact (see, for example, Genesis 29:25, Genesis 42:27). Pharaoh realized that this was a dream. But, then, most people realize they have been dreaming once they wake up. Why mention it?

An Answer: The first dream of cows eating cows, while very unusual, is not yet pure fantasy; cows, while not carnivorous, can be imagined eating other cows. It didn't appear to be as symbolic as the second dream was. But when he dreamt of the ears of corn eating other ears of corn he realized that this was certainly a fantasy. In no stretch of the imagination could one think this could happen in real life. So "behold Pharaoh had a dream" means that he had a dream in the true sense of the term — a dream with symbolic content. Such dreams, their symbolism, call for interpretation, because the dream can't be taken at face value.

It is for this reason that only after the second dream does Rashi tell us that it "need[ed] to be interpreted."

But what did Rashi mean by "a whole dream was completed before him"?

YOUR ANSWER:

FURTHER ANALYSIS OF RASHI'S WORDS _____

Answer: Here Rashi tells us that Pharaoh realized that the two dreams he had were really one. He now had a (single) whole, completed dream. This meant that the dream of the cows and that of the corn were one and the same dream. If they were one, we can now understand why the Torah doesn't say after Pharaoh's first dream, "Behold it was a dream," because it wasn't yet a (completed) dream. This answers our second question.

It should be noted that throughout the Torah, when similar events are repeated, as here with Pharaoh's two dreams, Rashi will often relate to any differences between the two accounts — but, as usual, without explicitly stating that this is the purpose of his comment.

The importance of Pharaoh's recognizing that his dream was one can be judged by Joseph's interpretation of the dreams. His very first words to Pharaoh were "The dream of Pharaoh is one . . ." (Genesis 41:25). Clearly this was crucial both in Joseph's ability to correctly interpret the dream and for Pharaoh to appreciate Joseph's wisdom.

A DEEPER LOOK _____

Rashi says that Pharaoh realized that his two dreams were actually one; as the words והנה חלום clearly imply. But we would ask: How did Pharaoh himself know this?

You might say this is obvious, but the midrash makes the point that all Pharaoh's wise men thought he had two different dreams. (See 41:8: "And none could interpret *them* unto Pharaoh.") How did Pharaoh know they were one dream?

YOUR ANSWER:

Answer: Your own experience should be your guide in this. If you forget a name and someone makes several suggestions, you'll know which ones are wrong and which one is the correct name. The paradox is that if you couldn't remember the name, how would you recognize it when you heard it! The answer is that our knowledge exists both on a conscious and on an unconscious level. We may not be consciously aware of information that we possess on an unconscious level. For modern man this is certainly no new revelation. Considering this, we can understand that Pharaoh might not understand the meaning of his dream on a conscious level, while on an unconscious level, he could sense that his two dreams were really one.

(See *Mesiach Ilmim; Be'er BaSadeh*)

This Rashi comment uses Targum Onkelos to clarify a grammatical point. And then some.

Genesis 41:38

ויאמר פרעה אל עבדיו הנמצא כזה איש אשר רוח אלוקים בו.

הנמצא כזה: הנשכח כדין? אם נלך ונבקשנו הנמצא כמוהו? הנמצא לשון תמהה וכו׳

Can we find one as this?: *Rashi:* (the Targum) Can we find one as this? If we go and we search for one could we find anyone like him? This is a question.

What would you ask?

YOUR QUESTION:

QUESTIONING RASHI

What is Rashi clarifying by his comment? What is bothering Rashi?

YOUR ANSWER:

WHAT IS BOTHERING RASHI?

An Answer: This is a grammatical matter. The word הנמצא is grammatically unclear. It can be translated in different ways.

1. First person plural active, as "can we find?"

as in Genesis 47:25

ויאמרו החיתנו **נמצא** חן בעיני אדני והיינו עבדים לפרעה.

And they said: You have saved our lives; **may we find**
favor in your eyes, my lord, and we will be servants to
Pharoah.

2. Third person past, or present, passive, as "Has he (it), been
found?"

as in Exodus 21:16

וגנב איש ומכרו **ונמצא** בידו מות יומת.

And he that steals a man and sells him and **he be found**
in his hand he shall surely be put to death.

Rashi wants to show which translation is the right one.

Understanding Rashi

Rashi is telling us that of the above possibilities, #1 is the correct interpretation. He refers to the Targum because these different possible meanings (which all use the same word in Hebrew) are translated differently
in Aramaic. The words in the Targum, הנשכח כדין, mean "can we find
one as this?"

Why does Rashi choose this translation?

Your Answer:

Support for Rashi's Interpretation

An Answer: This is not an easy one! The commentators on Rashi make several
suggestions. See the Ramban (discussed below). He agrees with
Rashi and explains his reason. If we analyze the context of
Pharaoh's statement we can see the reason for Rashi's choice.

Joseph had said (41:33): "Let Pharaoh look for a man who is understanding and wise." And just before our sentence (after Joseph tells
Pharoah what must be done) we are told, "The matter appeared good in
the eyes of Pharaoh and in the eyes of all his servants." Read the section.
What appeared good to Pharaoh?

Your Answer:

An Answer: The advice of Joseph to look for a wise and understanding man.

Seen in this light, with Pharoah's emphasis on finding the right man, we see why Rashi interpreted the word הנמצא as "Can we find . . .?" The other meanings of this word, "Does there exist such a man?" or "Has there ever existed such a man as this?" are both irrelevant and inconsistent with the context. Pharoah is not asking a hypothetical question, rather a very practical one: "If we go and we search for one can we find anyone like him?"

A CLOSER LOOK AT RASHI'S WORDS

See how Rashi makes his point. He wants to emphasize that the letter נ stands for the first person plural (we), so he repeats the נ three times: אם נלך ונבקשנה הנמצה . . .

Thus, both a contextual analysis as well as a close analysis of each word in Rashi's comment enables us to gain a deeper understanding of his meaning.

A FINAL THOUGHT

The student may ask: After all is said and done, the difference between the two possible interpretations isn't very significant. The story is not altered in any way by choosing one interpretation over the other. In blunt terms: What difference does it make? Why should Rashi trouble himself to give us p'shat and keep us from making a mistaken interpretation when it really makes no difference?

Here are two suggested answers to this question.

1. It does make a difference. The Ramban offers an explanation as to why Pharaoh spoke in the first person plural. According to the Ramban, he did this in order to involve his servants in the radical decision of appointing a lowly, despised Hebrew slave to the prestigious position of Viceroy of Egypt. In this way he would enlist their cooperation and neutralize their antagonism. So, according to this interpretation, there is a difference between the different possible translations of the word הנמצא.

2. But we should also realize that for Rashi the correct interpretation — whether of any practical significance or not — is justification enough. The words of the Torah have to be understood, every word and every nuance, if for no other reason than because they are the word of G-d.

(See Mizrachi)

Rashi solves an apparent contradiction in the text by sleuth-like logic.

Genesis 41:55

ותרעב כל ארץ מצרים ויצעק העם אל פרעה ללחם ויאמר פרעה
לכל מצרים לכו אל יוסף אשר יאמר לכם תעשו.

ותרעב כל ארץ מצרים: שהרקיבה תבואתם שאצרו חוץ משל
יוסף.

And all the land of Egypt was famished: *Rashi:* For all
the grain they had stored up rotted except that of Joseph.

Rashi tells us that the grain rotted. What would you ask of Rashi?

What else would you ask?

YOUR QUESTIONS:

QUESTIONING RASHI _____

Question: Our standard question: What is bothering Rashi? What in the text
prompts him to make this comment?

Another question: Where in the Torah is there even a hint that the
grain rotted? Remember, neither Rashi nor the midrash, which is
Rashi's source, would make such a statement unless there were
some basis for it in the words of the Torah.

Hint:

Look also at the adjoining sentences.

Do you have answers?

YOUR ANSWERS:

WHAT IS BOTHERING RASHI? _____

Answer: The two questions have one answer. The Torah tells us, immediately before this sentence, "In all the land of Egypt there was bread."
If there was bread in Egypt, how can there also be famine, as it
says here? That is what is bothering Rashi.

How does Rashi's comment deal with this?

YOUR ANSWER:

UNDERSTANDING RASHI

His explanation that there was grain but that it rotted explains the difficulty.

But we should ask: How does Rashi conclude that the grain of the individual Egyptians rotted?

If you think about it you can figure this out yourself.

YOUR ANSWER:

ANALYZING RASHI

Answer: There are two givens:

1. There was grain in Egypt (41:54), and

2. There was also famine and no grain as evidenced by the fact that the Egyptians had to ask Joseph for help (41:55).

We can add another thought. The Egyptians were fully aware that the seven years of plenty would be followed by seven years of famine. Isn't it reasonable to assume that the people would have stored up their own private provisions beyond what the state stored? Knowing human nature, we can confidently assume that they did save up some provisions. If so, what happened to them?

They must have rotted! There you have it.

(See Mizrachi)

Rashi makes us aware that we haven't fully understood the Torah verse. But first we must understand Rashi!

Genesis 42:23

והם לא ידעו כי שמע יוסף כי המליץ בינתם.

כי המליץ בינותם: כי כשהיו מדברים עמו היה המליץ ביניהם היודע לשון עברי ולשון מצרי והיה מליץ דבריהם ליוסף ודברי יוסף להם לכך היו סבורים שאין יוסף מכיר בלשון עברי.

For the interpreter was between them: *Rashi:* For when they had spoken to him there was an interpreter between them who knew the Hebrew language and the Egyptian language. He interpreted their words to Joseph and Joseph's words to them. Consequently they were under the impression that Joseph was not familiar with the Hebrew language.

What is your question on Rashi's comment?

Questioning Rashi

Rashi seems to be telling us what a מליץ is. He certainly could have told us that in much less words. Why is he belaboring the point? What is bothering him?

Hint:

Read the full Torah sentence again and ask yourself what it says.

והם לא ידעו כי שמע יוסף כי המליץ בינתם.
And they did not know that Joseph understood, because the translator was between them.

Does it make sense to you? What is bothering Rashi?

What Is Bothering Rashi?

Of course it doesn't make sense! *Because* the translator was between them they didn't think Joseph understood them? Quite the contrary, *only because* the translator was there could he understand what they were saying.

Now look at Rashi's comment and see how he explains away this question. Do you understand? What do you understand?

YOUR ANSWER:

UNDERSTANDING RASHI

Answer: By the addition of a word or two, Rashi solves the problem. Rashi says "When they *had spoken* to him there *was* a translator between them . . ." By placing the sentence in the past tense, Rashi avoids the confusion. The meaning now is: Since in previous conversations with Joseph the translator was present, they assumed that he didn't understand Hebrew. But now, when the translator was not present (for they weren't speaking to Joseph), they could speak freely among themselves.

Rashi's comment is a necessary explanation once we acquire his sensitivity to the demands of precision in the Torah's languauge.

(See Mizrachi)

This Rashi is an easy one. . . with some tough questions!

Genesis 42:27

ויפתח האחד את שקו לתת מספוא לחמרו במלון וירא את כספו
והנה הוא בפי אמתחתו.

ויפתח האחד: הוא לוי שנשאר יחיד משמעון בן זוגו.

And the one opened: *Rashi:* This was Levi who remained alone being without Simeon his companion.

What question would you ask?

YOUR QUESTION:

QUESTIONING RASHI

A Question: How does Rashi conclude that it was Levi? What is it about the verse that leads him to this?

WHAT IS BOTHERING RASHI?

Answer: The Hebrew has האחד, meaning "the one." It should have said

אחד, "one." The definite article הי means a special, particular one. Rashi wants to know: Which one? How does he conclude it was Levi?

YOUR ANSWER:

UNDERSTANDING RASHI

An Answer: Of the nine brothers returning to their father Jacob, Rashi chooses Levi as the one referred to here.

He also tells us why Levi is the likely one.

A LESSON IN RASHI'S METHOD

Rashi is quite alert to the use of the הי הידיעה, the definite article. If the Torah uses it, it should be clear what article is referred to. If it is not clear — as in this case, it wasn't clear who "the" one was — then Rashi will usually tell us what the הי הידיעה is referring to.

A DEEPER LOOK

We know that Joseph commanded his staff to return each brother's money in his bag (See 42:25). The other brothers only found their money after they returned home and emptied their bags (see 42:35). When they got to the inn, Levi opened his bag to feed his animal; the others certainly did likewise. Why, then, was it only Levi who found his money?

Hint:

Reread all the relevant sentences carefully.

YOUR ANSWER:

An Answer: Levi's money was at the top of his bag, at its opening (42:27), while the others found their money deeper inside their bags (42:35). So Levi saw the money immediately upon opening his bag, while the others could have taken out some grain in the inn, without yet discovering their money.

But that answer leads inevitably to another question.

What is the question?

An Even Deeper Look

A Question: Why did Joseph put only Levi's money on top of his bag, where he knew it would be found on the way? Why didn't he do this to the other brothers?

Can you suggest an answer?

Your Answer:

Analyzing Rashi

Answer: I would suggest the following. We know that Joseph had his filial difficulties only with Leah's sons. Remember that he got along with the maidservants' sons (see Genesis 37:2). Leah's sons were: Reuben, Simeon, Levi, Judah, Issachar and Zebulun.

Joseph looked for those responsible for his being sold into slavery.

He started with the eldest and worked his way down. The first born, Reuben, had already acquitted himself in Joseph's presence. (See above, 42:22, where he says: "Did I not say to you as follows, Do not sin against the child, but you didn't listen?") Next came Simeon. Joseph put him under house arrest. (Corroboration of this interpretation can be found in the *Ibn Ezra, Hizkuni* and *Bechor Shor*.) The next in line is Levi. This would explain why Levi was set up more than the others.

Do you have a better answer ?

(See *Mizrachi; Maharsha*)

Again, a close look at the words Rashi uses clues us in to the lesson in his comment.

Genesis 44:18

ויגש אליו יהודה ויאמר בי אדני ידבר נא עבדך דבר באזני אדני
ואל יחר אפך בעבדך כי כמוך כפרעה.

> **ויגש אליו וגו'. דבר באזני אדני:** יכנסו דברי באזניך.
>
> **Then Judah came near to him, etc ... A word in my lord's ears:** *Rashi:* May my words penetrate into your ears.

Note: Rashi quotes the first words of the *parshah* and then begins with the relevant *dibbur hamaschil*. The first Rashi comment of each *sedra* begins with the first words of the *sedra*, even if he doesn't actually comment on them, as in this case. This may be the work of an editor and not Rashi himself.

Do you have a question on this comment?

YOUR QUESTION:

QUESTIONING RASHI

We see that Rashi is reworking the *dibbur hamaschil*, from דבר באזני אדני to יכנסו דברי באזניך. Our question: Why is he doing this? It looks like a Type II comment — Rashi is warning us of a wrong interpretation. What wrong interpretation is he telling us to avoid?

YOUR ANSWER:

OF WHAT IS RASHI WARNING US? _____

An Answer: The words "Let your servant please speak a word in my lord's ears . . ."
             imply that Judah wants to speak with Joseph privately, just the
             two of them ("in my lord's ears"). But this can't be the meaning of
             his words. Why not?

YOUR ANSWER:

An Answer: Remember there was a translator between them (See 42:23); Jo-
             seph spoke Egyptian, and while the brothers spoke Hebrew, they
             thought Joseph didn't understand their language as they didn't
             understand his. So how could Judah speak privately, one to one,
             with Joseph, without an interpreter?

             So our initial understanding cannot be correct, because Judah could not
             talk directly to Joseph. What then does it mean?

RASHI'S REWORKING _____

The wrong interpretation is based on a misunderstanding, namely that
Judah's speaking באזני אדוני . . . ידבר נא will enter Joseph's ears. We are
misled both because of the words "may your servant speak . . . in my lord's
ears" and by the fact that Judah did step nearer to Joseph. Why else would
he step near if not to speak individually with him? But this is a wrong
conclusion for the reason stated above. To disabuse us of this idea, Rashi
adds the words יכנסו דברי. In doing this, Rashi is telling us that Judah is
pleading that his words (not his speaking) will enter Joseph's ears. This
is most reasonably interpreted to mean that he hopes Joseph will accept
what he has to say.

(See Sifsei Chachomim)

Occasionally the original wording of Rashi is in doubt. This comment provides such an example. We will analyze it in our usual way. Then we will compare the various editions.

Familiarity with Rashi's style enables us to make an educated guess as to the correct text.

Genesis 45:28

ויאמר ישראל רב עוד יוסף בני חי אלכה ואראנו בטרם אמות.

רב עוד: רב לי שמחה וחדוה הואיל ועוד יוסף בני חי.
A lot, much: *Rashi:* I have much joy and pleasure, since my son Joseph is still alive.

[Note: This may not be the text you will find in your Chumash. This will be discussed below.]

Your Question:

Questioning Rashi _____

Question: What is unclear here that Rashi needs to comment on? The sentence seems clear enough as it is.

What is bothering Rashi?

Hint:

The *dibbur hamaschil.*

Your Answer:

What Is Bothering Rashi? _____

An Answer: The *dibbur hamaschil* are רב עוד, meaning "a lot, many." This is a redundancy. A lot is many. Rashi wants to understand the meaning of these words in this sentence.

How does he do this? Analyze Rashi's comment closely and give

Your Answer:

117 —

ANALYZING RASHI

Rashi divides the sentence into two parts:

1. רב לי שמחה וחדוה, "I have much joy and pleasure."

2. הואיל ועוד יוסף בני חי, "since my son Joseph is still alive."

In this way he separates the word רב from the word עוד. He also gives the word עוד a different meaning; it doesn't mean "a lot," as we might have thought, rather it means "still."

Let's see how he does it.

Notice that Rashi adds several words to the Torah's words (remember a Type II comment). Which words does he add? Why?

YOUR ANSWER:

UNDERSTANDING RASHI

An Answer: He adds the words לי שמחה וחדוה after the word רב, thus separating it from the word עוד.

He adds the words שמחה וחדוה to explain what it is that is רב, "much." Thus the word רב means "I have much joy and pleasure."

He adds the word הואיל, "since," to connect the two parts of the sentence.

Rashi is rejecting the translation: "It is more than enough (רב עוד), that Joseph my son is alive." Remember, they told Jacob: "Joseph is yet alive and he is ruler over Egypt." Jacob could be saying: It is more than enough that he is alive — who cares if he is ruler or not! This is the interpretation of Rashbam. But Rashi rejects this interpretation.

His interpretation tells us that the sentence means: "Much joy and pleasure are mine since Joseph my son is still alive."

Can you see why Rashi selects his interpretation and rejects the other one ?

YOUR ANSWER:

SUPPORT FOR RASHI'S INTERPRETATION

An Answer: Rashi rejects putting the words רב עוד together. His guide here is the musical notes (*trop*) under the words. There is only one note under the two words עוד יוסף, meaning they are joined. Notice that the words עוד-יוסף have a hyphen (*makaf*) connecting them. This would indicate that עוד goes together with the latter part of the sentence and not with the word רב.

A Closer Look

The correct wording of this comment is in doubt. Different Chumashim have slightly different *dibbur hamaschil* and comment. Since every word in Rashi is crucial to the correct understanding, it is important to know what Rashi actually wrote. How can we determine this? This is really a job for scholars who can compare manuscripts and editions, not for the average student. But let's take a brief excursion into this esoteric area of the "science of Rashi." We will see that having a "feel" for Rashi's style of interpretation helps us arrive at the most reasonable guess as to Rashi's original words.

Analyzing Rashi — Discovering the Correct Text

Rashi wrote long before the printing press (or desktop publishing!) was invented. His original manuscript is lost. Were such a manuscript to be found, it would be worth millions of dollars. There are three main ancient printings of Rashi's commentary that are used as standards.

The Various Texts of This Rashi

Following are the three main texts of Rashi on this sentence, as they are found in the various ancient prints. Notice the differences between them both in the *dibbur hamaschil* and in the comment itself.

1) **רב לי.** עוד שמחה וחדוה הואיל וייסף בני חי (1475) Regio.

2) **רב עוד יוסף בני חי.** רב לי שמחה וחדוה הואיל ועוד יוסף בני חי (1470) Rome.

3) **רב עוד יוסף.** רב לי עוד שמחה וחדוה הואיל ועוד יוסף בני חי (1476) Alkabetz.

Which text would you assume is the REAL Rashi? Let me say that the commentators on Rashi are in serious debate as to the correct reading, so do not feel embarrassed if the task looks overwhelming. How could you ever know, you may ask. But if you do have a guess, write it out together with your reasoning.

Your Answer:

Analyzing Rashi's Words

We will approach this from several angles.

Rashi's Style

Rashi always writes in a way that clarifies matters for the student and not in a way that might confuse him. Notice that in the Alkabetz edition the word עוד is written twice. This has given the commentators a hard time. Why use it twice? What in the Torah's words justifies the repetition of this word? This only leads to confusion. This is not Rashi's way. So the text that has the word only once seems truer to Rashi's spirit (see *Mizrachi*).

The Musical Notes

As we mentioned above, the musical notes under the words indicate that the two words רב and עוד have to be separated. The Rome Edition does this most clearly (*Yosef Hallel*).

Onkelos and Rashi

Another clue is to see the Targum Onkelos on this sentence. As we have seen many times, Rashi goes in his footsteps. Look at the Targum. What do you see?

An Answer: Onkelos writes: ואמר ישראל סגי לי חדוא עד כען יוסף ברי קים.

Translated it means, "And Israel said: I have great joy, my son Joseph is still alive." As you can see this is strikingly close to Rashi. To which of the three editions above is this Onkelos similar?

Your Answer:

An Answer: The Rome printing is closest. Again the word עוד is the key here. The Rome edition uses it only in the second half of the comment — just as Onkelos does when he writes עד כען יוסף בני חי — and not twice like the Alkabetz edition.

In the Regio edition, the word עוד is used only once, but in the first part of the sentence, not as in Onkelos which has it in the second part of the sentence.

In summary: It would seem that Rashi actually wrote what we have in the Rome Edition. It makes most sense, its meaning is clearest and it follows the Targum very closely. In spite of all this, most Chumashim that you will pick up will not have the Rashi this way!

(See *Mizrachi; Yosef Hallel*)

❖ ❖ ❖

A close reading of the sentence shows how Rashi's interpretation has a firm anchor in text.

Genesis 46:4

אנכי ארד עמך מצרימה ואנכי אעלך גם עלה ויוסף ישית ידו על עיניך.

ואנכי אעלך: הבטיחו להיות נקבר בארץ.
And I shall also surely bring you up: *Rashi:* He promised him that he would be buried in Eretz [Yisroel]."

What would you ask Rashi here?

YOUR QUESTION:

QUESTIONING RASHI

One question we can ask is: How does Rashi know this? How does he know that G-d is promising Jacob that he will be buried in Israel? We would expect a more optimistic promise — that Jacob will be returned to Eretz Yisroel while still alive. How does Rashi know that this was not the promise? What in the text is bothering Rashi ?

WHAT IS BOTHERING RASHI?

An Answer: G-d says to Jacob: "I will go down *with* you . . . . And I will bring you up." These are not parallel phrases. It should have said ". . . and I will go up with you." This change in language is what is bothering Rashi.

How does he deal with this ?

YOUR ANSWER:

UNDERSTANDING RASHI

An Answer: "Going up" and "going down" are terms for coming to or leaving Eretz Yisroel (see Rashi, Genesis 45:9). So when G-d says that He'll "bring up," He means He will return Jacob to Eretz Yisroel. Jacob went down to Egypt on his own power and thus it says G-d went *with* him. But on his return, G-d says "I will bring you up," meaning the return will not be by Jacob's own power; rather after his death, G-d will bring him up to be buried.

(See Maskil L'Dovid)

This is one of many Rashi comments that provide us with maxims. Many have entered common usage because Rashi made them known.

Genesis 47:31

ויאמר השבעה לי וישבע לו וישתחו ישראל על ראש המטה.

וישתחו ישראל: תעלה בעידניה סגיד ליה.
And Israel prostrated himself: *Rashi:* (A proverb says) "when the fox has his time, bow down to him."

What exactly does this saying mean here?

YOUR ANSWER:

THE RELEVANCE OF THE PROVERB

The proverb says that the fox, who is one of the smaller, weaker animals, may also have his hour in the sun, his time of supremacy. At that time it is wise and fitting to respect him (bow down to him) in spite of his ordinarily lesser position. Joseph, who is Jacob's son, should show his father respect, not the other way around. Nevertheless, at this time he commands respect from Jacob, since Joseph is Viceroy of Egypt and only he can fulfill his father's request to be buried in Eretz Yisroel. It is for this reason that Jacob bows to his son Joseph.

The meaning is clear. Here Rashi is neither answering a question nor steering us away from a possible misunderstanding. He furnishes us with a Talmudic maxim which puts the unusual act of Jacob's bowing down to his own son, in context.

But we would ask:

Why didn't Rashi make this same comment when Joseph's older brothers bowed down to him (see 42:6)?

YOUR ANSWER:

UNDERSTANDING RASHI _____

Several answers can be offered. The most obvious is that the brothers didn't know that the Viceroy before whom they stood was their younger brother Joseph.

❖ ❖ ❖

A puzzling Rashi comment gives us insight into a principle for understanding his comments.

Genesis 48:16

המלאך הגאל אותי מכל רע יברך את הנערים ויקרא בהם שמי
ושם אבותי אברהם ויצחק וידגו לרב בקרב הארץ.

 יברך את הנערים: מנשה ואפרים.
He shall bless the lads: *Rashi:* Menasseh and Ephraim.

What would you ask on this comment?

YOUR QUESTION:

QUESTIONING RASHI _____

This question should be easy: What is Rashi telling us? Certainly we know that "the lads" refers to Joseph's sons Menasseh and Ephraim! The whole chapter speaks only about them. Why is Rashi telling us the obvious?

This brief comment looks like a Type II comment, one meant to help us avoid a misunderstanding. Clearly he wants us to know that "the lads" does not refer to some other boys. But to whom else could "the lads" refer?

YOUR ANSWER:

What Misunderstanding

This is really a difficult one! The foremost commentators on Rashi give differing explanations for this puzzling comment. Let's look at them.

The *Mizrachi* suggests that Rashi needs to tell us that "the lads" refers to Ephraim and Menasseh since we might have thought otherwise. We might have thought that these are some other children, because later on (verse 20) it says that Jacob explicitly blessed Ephraim and Menasseh ("and he blessed them that day saying . . ."). Thus, our verse might possibly refer to some other of Joseph's children, perhaps to those too young to visit Jacob. The *Mizrachi* goes on to explain that this, however, is a mistaken assumption, since our verse is introduced by (verse 15) saying, "And he blessed Joseph and he said . . ." This clearly means Joseph's children, Ephraim and Menasseh.

The *Gur Aryeh* takes a very different view. He explains the need for Rashi's comment as follows. Our verse is introduced by (verse 15) which says, "And he blessed Joseph . . ." and *not* Ephraim and Menasseh. Thus we might have thought that these "lads" refer to some other children of Joseph, those perhaps to be born in the future.

The Misunderstanding: Reasonable or Unreasonable?

These two interpretations are not just different, they are diametrically opposed to each other. Notice that the *Mizrachi* and the *Gur Aryeh* cite the same verse 15, but to prove opposite points! When we have commentators proving their point in a way that can be used to show just the opposite position, the cogency of each position is considerably weakened.

We must assume that if Rashi comes to guide us away from a possible misunderstanding, then that misunderstanding should be a likely and reasonable one, not a dubious, debatable one. For this reason it is difficult to accept the interpretations of the *Mizrachi* or the *Gur Aryeh*.

In fact, the *Sefer Zikaron* acknowledges the difficulty with this Rashi-comment and concedes that he can find no reasonable explanation for it. He leaves us with an unanswered question.

A Clue to Understanding Rashi

A very helpful method when trying to understand Rashi's Chumash commentary is to compare his comment with midrashim on the verse. When writing his commentary, Rashi had the world of midrash in front of him. He was conversant with both the Babylonian and the Jerusalem Talmuds, and with the midrashim on the Torah. We have been stressing throughout this book that frequently Rashi's comment is addressed to some difficulty in the Torah verse itself, but there are occasionally instances when he has in mind a midrash on the passage. Rashi's audience was familiar with the midrashim, and sometimes his intent is to show the preference of *p'shat* over *drash* in interpreting a particular phrase. When confronted with a difficult Rashi it may be helpful to see what the midrash has to say on the verse.

THE MIDRASH ON "THE LADS"

In Midrash *Bereishis Rabbah* (97:3) we find the following:

"He shall bless the lads": This is Joshua and Gideon.

On the face of it, an amazing midrash. Are we to believe that Jacob had Joshua (Moses' assistant and successor) and Gideon (one of the first judges of Israel) in mind, when blessing his son Joseph? They weren't even born yet!

But the commentaries on the midrash give us insight here. Notice the following points that tie both Joshua and Gideon to Jacob's blessing.

• What tribe does Joshua come from? And Gideon?

For your answer look at Bamidbar 13:8 and at the Book of Judges 6:15.

What did you find?

YOUR ANSWER:

Answer: Joshua is from the tribe of Ephraim and Gideon from the tribe of Menasseh!

• Jacob says, " The Angel redeeming me from all evil . . ."

Regarding Joshua, note what it says in the Book of Joshua 5:13–14. And regarding Gideon, note what it says in the Book of Judges 6:12 ff.

What did you find?

YOUR ANSWER:

Answer: In both cases these men are confronted by an Angel of G-d who comes to save them!

• Jacob says, "he shall bless the lads."

Regarding Joshua, see Exodus 33:11. Regarding Gideon, see Judges 6:15.

What did you find?

YOUR ANSWER:

Answer: We see that both are young men ("lads"). Joshua is explicitly called a "lad," while Gideon says he is the youngest in his father's house.

So we see that in three instances both Joshua and Gideon have points in common with Jacob's blessing. One could certainly be forgiven for thinking that perhaps Jacob's blessing does, in fact, have a prophetic ring and refers to these future leaders of Israel. While this is a *drash*, it is close enough to *p'shat* that one might be inclined to accept it as a reasonable interpretation.

RASHI'S PREFERENCE: CONTEXT OVER CONCEPT

Rashi, is in effect saying "I know the midrash says that these lads refer to Joshua and Gideon, but the *p'shat* interpretation here is that Jacob was referring to his immediate grandchildren, Menasseh and Ephraim." Rashi shows us that the total context of this verse — Joseph's bringing his two sons to see their grandfather, Jacob — is the basis for deciding the *p'shat*-level interpretation. The conceptual similarities that Joshua and Gideon share with Jacob's blessings point to a different level of interpretation — the midrashic interpretation.

(See *Mizrachi; Gur Aryeh; Sefer Zikaron; Tiferes Yoseph*)

Rashi's use of Onkelos obviates a difficulty in the Torah text.

Genesis 49:25

מֵאֵל אָבִיךָ וְיַעְזְרֶךָּ וְאֵת שַׁדַּי וִיבָרְכֶךָּ בִּרְכֹת שָׁמַיִם מֵעָל בִּרְכֹת תְּהוֹם רֹבֶצֶת תָּחַת בִּרְכֹת שָׁדַיִם וָרָחַם.

בּרְכַת שָׁדַיִם וָרָחַם: בִּרְכָתָא דְאַבָּא וְדְאִמָּא. כְּלוֹמַר, יִתְבָּרְכוּ הַמּוֹלִידִים וְהַיּוֹלְדוֹת, שֶׁיְּהִיוּ הַזְּכָרִים מַזְרִיעִין טִפָּה הָרְאוּיָה לְהֵרָיוֹן, וְהַנְּקֵבוֹת לֹא יְשַׁכְּלוּ אֶת רֶחֶם שֶׁלָּהֶן לְהַפִּיל עוּבְּרֵיהֶן.

Blessings of the breasts and of the womb: *Rashi:* [Onkelos renders this] blessings for father and for mother. That is to say, may those who father and those who give birth be blessed; that the males should inseminate with a drop which is fit for conception and the females should not bereave their wombs, by miscarrying their fetuses.

An obvious question arises here. What is it?

YOUR QUESTION:

QUESTIONING RASHI

Question: Why does Rashi twist the words out of their simple meaning? The Hebrew word שדים usually means "breasts." Why does Rashi (and Onkelos) reinterpret the word to mean just the opposite, "father"?

Can you figure out what is bothering Rashi? The answer is based on logic, not on some hidden message.

YOUR ANSWER:

WHAT IS BOTHERING RASHI?

Answer: If the correct meaning of שדים were "breasts," and the phrase was a blessing only for woman, the word order should have been reversed. It should have been "womb and breasts," since pregnancy (womb) comes before nursing (breasts)!

How does Rashi's interpretation meet this need?

YOUR ANSWER:

Understanding Rashi

Rashi sought a meaning for שדים that would allow the order of the words to make sense. He found that the Hebrew root שד could also mean "to shoot" (to inseminate). Thus it could refer to the male (father) who inseminates the womb.

Analyzing Rashi

Rashi uses the word כלומר, "that is to say." This usually means that he is clearing up a possible misunderstanding. In this case the misunderstanding could be that the words "father and mother" in the Onkelos might be interpreted to mean that the blessings come from the father and mother. Therefore Rashi clarifies the point: the parents are on the receiving end of the blessings and are not the givers.

(See *Be'er Yitzchak; L'Phshuto shel Rashi*)

Watch how this Rashi comment unfolds under analysis to reveal its complex message.

Genesis 50: 19–20

ויאמר אלהם יוסף אל תיראו כי התחת אלוקים אני. ואתם חשבתם עלי רעה אלוקים חשבה לטבה למען עשה כיום הזה להחיות עם רב.

כי התחת אלוקים אני: שמא במקומו אני, בתמיה. אם הייתי רוצה להרע לכם כלום אני יכול, והלא אתם כולכם חשבתם עלי רעה והקב"ה חשבה לטובה, והאיך אני לבדי יכול להרע לכם.

For am I instead of G‑d?: *Rashi:* Am I, perhaps, in His stead? [The ה expresses] a question. Even if I wished to do you harm would I be able to? For did you not, all of you, think to do me evil but the Holy One, Blessed be He, planned it for good. How then can I, alone, do evil to you?

Comparing Rashi's Comment with the Torah Verse

Let us start questioning Rashi by comparing his words with those of the Torah. Look closely at the Rashi comment and again at the verse in the Torah. What changes, substitutions and/or additions does Rashi make to the text?

129 —

Write them out:

1.

2.

3.

Rashi's Reworking of the Text _____

Did you notice these?:

1. He exchanges שמא for כי.

2. He exchanges במקומו for התחת.

3. He connects sentence 19 with 20.

4. He adds the words, "Even if I wished to do you harm, would I be able to?" and places them between the two sentences.

5. He inserts the word כלכם between the words אתם חשבתם.

Now, why does he do all this? What is bothering him?

Your Answer:

What Is Bothering Rashi? _____

Answers: 1. When you read Joseph's statement as a question and translate the word כי as "because" (as it is usually translated), there is a difficulty. "Because" usually introduces an answer to a question, yet here it introduces the question itself! The Hebrew word כי (as "because") doesn't fit with the ה' השאלה. How can that be explained?

2. Sentence 20 begins with the word "And" Why does it? In what way is it connected to the previous verse?

3. At first glance, it is difficult to see the connection between sentence 20 and Joseph's rhetorical question, "Am I perhaps in G-d's place?" What has the fact that the brothers intended to do Joseph harm have to do with Joseph's attempt to calm their fears. Quite the contrary! By reminding the brothers of their evil plans towards him, he would increase their fears of retribution.

4. The word אתם, "you" plural in the phrase אתם חשבתם is redundant, since חשבתם alone means "you planned . . ." Why is it there?

5. An additional point to note: The Targum, with which Rashi was familiar, paraphrases Joseph's statement as follows: "Fear not.

Because I am subservient to [under] G-d." The Targum thus translates the word תחת as "under" and not as "in place of." He also disregards the הי השאלה, not taking Joseph's words as a question.

Rashi disagrees with the Targum on both counts.

How does Rashi's reworking of the sentence deal with these questions?

YOUR ANSWER:

UNDERSTANDING RASHI

1. By translating כי as "perhaps" (and not "because") he has overcome the contradiction between the הי השאלה (a question) and the word "because." "Perhaps" fits very well with a rhetorical question.

2. By translating the Hebrew התחת to mean "in His place" and not "under Him," Rashi has clarified its meaning (in opposition to the Targum's translation).

3. Rashi connects the two sentences (and comments on both of them under one *dibbur hamaschil*), by showing that the second sentence is an explanation of the first. By adding the words "Even if I wished to do you harm . . .," Rashi bridges the two sentences and shows how their fears are ungrounded. Joseph is saying that even if he wished to harm them, he wouldn't succeed as they hadn't succeeded in harming him.

4. Rashi stresses that the words "you, all of you, do me evil . . ." are intended to point out the impossibility of Joseph's harming them. They, all of them, tried to harm him and failed, so how could Joseph alone succeed in harming them? In this way Rashi has artfully dealt with the apparently superfluous word ואתם.

A CLOSER LOOK AT RASHI'S WORDS

Notice that Rash points out the contra positions of "all of you" versus "I" alone. Notice also that these two words are back to back in the Torah; the "I" is the last word of sentence 19 while "You" is the first word in sentence 20. Rashi is telling us that the word order in the Torah is meant to emphasize this dichotomy.

(See Rashi HaShalem)

About the Author

Avigdor Bonchek has Rabbinic ordination from Ner Israel Rabbinical College of Baltimore and a doctorate in clinical psychology from New York Univ. He has taught Torah studies at the Ohr Somyach Center for Judaic Studies in Jerusalem. He has been a lecturer of psychological courses at the Hebrew University of Jerusalem for the past 25 years. Previously he taught at the City University of New York, Yeshiva University and Ben Gurion University in Israel. Dr. Bonchek is a practicing psychotherapist. His book *The Problem Student: A Cognitive/ Behavioral Approach* has been published in Hebrew. His book *Studying the Torah: A Guide to In-Depth Interpretation* has been published by Jason Aronson Publishers. Dr. Bonchek lives in Jerusalem with his wife, Shulamis, and their six children.